S0-ADV-694

donuts

AN AMERICAN PASSION

ALSO BY JOHN T. EDGE

Fried Chicken: An American Story
Apple Pie: An American Story
Hamburgers & Fries: An American Story

donuts

AN AMERICAN PASSION

John T. Edge

G. P. PUTNAM'S SONS

NEW YORK

G. P. PUTNAM'S SONS
Publishers Since 1838
Published by the Penguin Group
Penguin Group (USA) Inc., 375 Hudson Street, New York, New York 10014, USA •
Penguin Group (Canada), 90 Eglinton Avenue, Suite 700, Toronto, Ontario M4P 2Y3, Canada
(a division of Pearson Penguin Canada Inc.) • Penguin Books Ltd, 80 Strand, London
WC2R 0RL, England • Penguin Ireland, 25 St Stephen's Green, Dublin 2, Ireland
(a division of Penguin Books Ltd) • Penguin Group (Australia), 250 Camberwell Road,
Camberwell, Victoria 3124, Australia (a division of Pearson Australia Group Pty Ltd) •
Penguin Books India Pvt Ltd, 11 Community Centre, Panchsheel Park,
New Delhi–110 017, India • Penguin Group (NZ), Cnr Airborne and Rosedale Roads,
Albany, Auckland 1310, New Zealand (a division of Pearson New Zealand Ltd) •
Penguin Books (South Africa) (Pty) Ltd, 24 Sturdee Avenue, Rosebank,
Johannesburg 2196, South Africa

Penguin Books Ltd, Registered Offices:
80 Strand, London WC2R 0RL, England

Library of Congress Cataloging-in-Publication Data

Edge, John T.
Donuts : an American passion / John T. Edge.
p.   cm.
ISBN 0-399-15358-6
1. Doughnuts.   I. Title
TX770.D67E44   2006   2005058682
641.8'653—dc22

Printed in the United States of America
1   3   5   7   9   10   8   6   4   2

Book design by Stephanie Huntwork

he doughnut is the dumb blonde of the pastry world. Buoyant and pillowy as a breast implant.

—JILL LIGHTNER, *Seattle Weekly*

he donut is the street thug of the pastry world, strutting past Madeleine and Éclair.

—PATRIC KUH, *Los Angeles* magazine

Contents

California Dalliance

New Traditionalists

The Future

Series Introduction

This is the final in a four-book series that celebrates America's iconic foods. Fried chicken led off; then, in quick succession, came apple pie and hamburgers. Now donuts. To my mind, these are small-*d* democratic foods that conjure our collective childhood and call to mind the question once posed by a Chinese philosopher: "What is patriotism, but nostalgia for the foods of our youth?"

I chose these foods because they transcend interregional variation and internecine debate about origin. Recognized from the Atlantic to the Pacific as uniquely American, they evoke the culinary and cultural fabric of our nation.

Though the places profiled and the recipes detailed can be read as keys to good eats, my intent was not to compile a list of the country's top spots. Instead, in this book and the ones that accompany it, I strive to showcase a crazy quilt of American passions.

Conflicted About
Krispy Kreme

the date is October 24, 2001. My fax machine unspools a note from Peter McKee, a Seattle friend, annotated with an article from his local alternative weekly. The city is six days shy of its first Krispy Kreme store and Peter, who came to love the yeast-raised rounds while working as a legal aid attorney in 1970s Georgia, is atwitter. He has begun cloaking himself in the goods of the brand. He has a T-shirt blazoned with green and red Krispy Kreme cursive. And he possesses a Krispy Kreme hat, one of those paper skiffs imprinted with the exuberant company logo.

Peter is a man obsessed. His enthusiasm is guileless, infectious. But unlike some of his fellow citizens, he understands the cultural clash signaled by Krispy Kreme's arrival. Along the bottom of an article from the *Seattle Weekly* entitled "Screw

Krispy Kreme," Peter scrawled his own analysis: "The back-lash has begun!"

Jill Lightner, author of the article, sees the arrival of Krispy Kreme as indicative of an American tendency toward "brand over product and conformity over quality." She argues that Seattle possesses its own donut culture. Why fall for some import? "Krispy Kreme offers a consistently adequate product throughout the country," writes Lightner, "and as of 5:30 a.m. on October 30, Seattleites will be lining up to receive their doses of fresh, hot adequacy."

Lightner's question is one of provincial pride. She wonders what's to keep Krispy Kreme from goose-stepping across the continent, wrecking mom and pop donut shops, paving the hinterlands with official-issue Winston-Salem glaze. Her implied patsy is a nation of lemmings posed as gourmands, standing in line at 5:30 in the morning for models of throughput, mass-produced donuts.

Over the course of a couple years of fried dough eating, I will discover that Lightner is not alone. Donuts, it seems, are not defined solely by sweetness and light. Love them a little too much, and people question your devotion. Fetishize them, and people question your discernment.

What's more, I will learn that no donut company is as proficient at cultivating devotion as Krispy Kreme. From 1996, when Krispy Kreme opened a retail store in Manhattan and Roy Blount, Jr., laid it on thick for *The New York Times Magazine*, declaring that "they are to other doughnuts what angels are to people," through 2004, when fried-dough fatigue set in and Krispy Kreme's stock price began to tank, the company appeared an unstoppable cultural and culinary force.

There were, of course, signs of ambiguity, of weakness. Blount may have foretold the company's Roman-candle rise and demise when he wrote, "I hope New York's acceptance of Krispy Kreme is not ironic. . . . Like life, a hot Krispy Kreme goes by so fast that if your tongue's in your cheek, you miss something."

Blount was addressing the perils of faddishness, the pitfalls of adopting style over substance. Or maybe Blount was goading us. Perhaps he intuited that, in the same manner Starbucks catalyzed patrons of our nation's local coffee shops, the grand opening of each new Krispy Kreme would sweep a klieg across the rabble of America's independent donut shops, bringing into relief the differences between homespun institutions and slick corporate edifices.

It's February of 2003. Pastry chef Ann Amernick of Washington, D.C., a veteran of the White House kitchens, knows how to read the nation's pulse by way of its cravings. And she doesn't like what she sees.

I arrive at her Cleveland Park shop, intent upon a donut, preferably one of those raspberry jelly ones I read about in *The Washington Post.* But I arrive too late in the day to purchase one of her beauties. Besides, she quit the raspberry jelly donuts a few months back, when the lines got long, the crowds unruly. Amernick is also out of Maryland strudel, a featherweight pastry burdened by apricots and currants, strafed with cinnamon. Although I did not seek her out to discuss America's burgeoning fascination with donuts, that's what she's serving.

"Krispy Kreme turned all this into a big deal," says Amernick, clad in a pressed white apron. "They've minted this brand of people that don't have a mind of their own," she says, her aquiline nose flaring. "They've somehow been conditioned to think of donuts as a rare commodity. They thrive on being told they can't have something. They shake their fists through the windows, cursing. All for donuts."

She reaches for a sugar cookie, turning it in her hand like a jewel. "I want to tell these people, 'Taste this cookie, this is my aunt's cookie,'" Amernick says. "But they want donuts, donuts, donuts. These people have lost their sense of discovery; they're following the lead of the press. They gobble my donuts like heathens and then tell me how they compare to Krispy Kreme. They don't understand that what makes my donuts light is the care with which they are made, the heart I pour into every one. They don't understand that these donuts began their life in something other than a machine. And that makes me sad."

Perhaps Amernick protests too much. But in her screed I hear something familiar, a tale of America's conflicted love affair with donuts. We love them dearly and, knowing this, loathe ourselves.

For the moment, let's set aside issues of health and allow

that, compared with, say, oat bran muffins, donuts are not the centerpieces of a cardiologist-endorsed twenty-first-century breakfast. Instead, let's focus upon the form. We food fetishists rhapsodize about the symmetry, about the perfectly round figure of a mass-produced donut. And then we recoil upon realizing that, by way of these rhapsodies, we define ourselves as complicit cogs in the machine of homogeneity.

Such as this is the burden of Krispy Kreme. We love them because they do their job so well. We loathe them for the same reason. But I have gleaned another way to understand the modern American donut ethic, one in which the ascendance of Krispy Kreme is affirming and catalytic. My son, Jess, showed me the way.

The date is June 25, 2005. The boom is over. Earlier this year, Enron veteran Stephen Cooper took over the reins of Krispy Kreme. Accusations of accounting irregularities swirl. This week, six directors of the Krispy Kreme corporation resigned from their positions. The bust has come.

Jess and I sit at a rickety table in Shipley Do-Nuts, the recently opened Oxford, Mississippi, branch of a Texas-born chain. New Krispy Kreme shops boast Doughnut Theaters, the workings of which compel children of all ages to gaze as circles of fried dough inch by on a conveyor belt, emerging first from a bath in hot oil, then from a shower of glaze.

Shipley, however, is comparatively low-rent. There are no automated conveyor belts, no theater. Just a proofing box, a couple of deep fryers, and a crew of three working in a cloud of flour. My friends who were born and raised in Oxford tell me that this is the second Shipley incarnation. They say that through the 1970s there was another Shipley, and their donuts were good, but that the cooks staked a claim to local fame by way of chili and fried chicken.

As we wait at the counter, I tell four-year-old Jess about the old Shipley. And he asks the obvious question, "Did they put glaze on the fried chicken?" I tell him that although I am familiar with honey-drizzled fried chicken, I doubt that Shipley ever sugar-glazed its birds. But Jess is having none of that. The idea is fixed in his head. As he reaches for his prize he asks, "Doesn't Krispy Kreme have glazed chicken?" Like many donut fans, Jess ascribes all that is good to Krispy Kreme. And in his book, glazed fried chicken is good.

There's a glimmer of logic in his fixation, for were it not for the Krispy Kreme fad, our town probably would not have a Shipley Do-Nut shop. I tell him as much, explaining that the interest in Krispy Kreme reinvigorated the likes of Shipley. But my donut-wonk talk bores Jess. Instead of listening, he decamps from our table, donut in hand, and climbs a red plywood proscenium to get a better view of the kitchen that gave birth to his yeast-raised prize.

becoming
american

f ried chicken and hamburgers and apple pie are American by evolution. With donuts, on the other hand, you can track the transition from *other* to *ours* as a three-step public relations campaign. And although the players have not always been in cahoots, their work has often proved complementary. Call this a three-round history of the donut:

Round one was about motherhood. At a time when the Salvation Army was searching for ways to brand itself as American, operatives in World War I France seized upon the donut. Soon, comely Salvationists in tin hats were smiling for the cameras and tending vats of roiling lard. As they dipped donuts for their boys, they dispensed motherhood. By the close of World War I, the Salvation Army was among the strongest charitable forces in America—and their chosen totem, the donut, was an ingrained symbol of home.

Round two was about modernity. Adolph Levitt, a Jew from Eastern Europe, applied the industrial model of efficiency to donuts. In 1921, when homogenization was the watchword, he devised a machine and a mix to sell to returning veterans. He called it the Wonderful Almost Human Doughnut Machine, and, when filled with his proprietary dough mix, it cranked out hundreds of perfectly round donuts per hour. Placed in a window for all to see, the machine stopped traffic in Times Square.

Round three was about glamour. Donuts were a plebian dish, affordable for all. But, in the 1920s, as the nation slid into an economic depression, the industry feared that donuts might go the way of the street corner apple. So they aligned themselves with America's emerging aristocracy, the ladies and gentlemen of Hollywood. Among the highlights: Stan Laurel of Laurel and Hardy fame posed for the paparazzi while holding a donut high. Shirley Temple starred in a short, *Dora's Dunking Donuts*. And director Frank Capra incorporated donut scenes into his films, most famously *It Happened One Night*, wherein a working stiff (Clark Gable) teaches an heiress (Claudette Colbert) donut etiquette.

To the public of the day, the donut seemed kismet. A cynic would say that such synergies were nothing more than donut industry–funded product placements. But cynics, at least the most quarrelsome kind, are bores.

Get the Lead Out

n ew England is the likely American beachhead of fried dough. But don't be so bold as to posit that, west of the Mississippi, donuts are a newfangled food that came to popularity in the early years of the twentieth century. You won't be in a good position to defend yourself, not if you take into account reports of Fisherman's Wharf donuts from 1850s California and of lumber camp donuts from 1870s Oregon, and most certainly not if you consider Little Pittsburgh Doughnuts, long popular in the mining camp of Leadville, Colorado.

According to Jessup Whitehead's *The Hotel Book of Bread and Cakes*, published in 1882, and based on reporting from the *Chicago Daily National Hotel Reporter*, the lard-fried rings became popular when "Leadville first began grinding in crowds of mining men poor, and grinding them out rich." Searching for a cheap way to feed these men, camp bakeries settled upon donuts and began to advertise them by way of one- and two-line inserts in the local papers.

It seemed, wrote a correspondent for the *Hotel Reporter*, as if "all the news in town was gathered for the express purpose of drawing attention to doughnuts." Whitehead's book includes this remarkable report: "Our esteemed fellow citizen fell down a shaft 500 feet deep, last evening. He struck on his head and probably never knew what hurt him." And as a coda, "O! those Little Pittsburgh doughnuts are so very fine, if you try them once, you'll buy them every time, at the Union Bakery."

ONE

Going Dutch:
The Early Years

i'm a sucker for old newspaper clips, a geek bent on under-standing America by way of the stories we tell about one another. I'm especially keen on vitriol and editorial bluster. Case in point: "The American doughnut is but a degenerate Dutch olykoeck," wrote Eunice Barnard in a 1930s *New York Times* dispatch, "with a yawning hole where once a nut or raisin was embedded in a luscious center."

Barnard was justified in tracing the birth of the donut be-yond these shores. And her aim toward Holland was true. But no matter how much I admire her pluck, the claim of degen-eracy is a matter of some debate. Most historians believe that the Dutch were the first to arrive here in great numbers with a taste and a talent for fried dough. (Of course, there are lesser schools of thought that claim, for instance, a Native

American birth for donuts and cite petrified specimens retrieved from an Oklahoma cave as proof.) The truth is that
fried pastries are universal. They are historical. They are even
biblical. Chapter seven, verse twelve of Leviticus prescribes
that offerings of thanksgiving to God be made of "cakes min-
gled with oil, of fine flour, fried."

Do a little digging about in bakery archives, and you'll
learn that the Celts claim fried cakes as their own and have
long served them on All Hallows' Eve. Just as Italians dote
on *zeppole* and dish them on St. Joseph's Day. And South
Africans dip *koeksister*, braids of fried dough, in simple syrup
all year long.

And then there are *loukoumades*, the honey-swabbed fritters of Greece; *jakeli*, the saffron-tinged, corn syrup–enrobed
fry breads of India; *awwamaat*, a Lebanese fried dough,
coated in nuts; and *krafne*, a yeast-risen and brandy-spiked fry
bread popular in Croatia. And don't forget *pètes de nonne*, the
French contribution to the world of fried dough, which translates as "nun's farts." Not to be outdone, the Pennsylvania
Dutch have long served *paffefatzle*, or "preacher's farts."

All of which is to say that I can, with a reasonable degree
of conviction, proclaim that the donut is not endemic to
America. The task that proves most difficult, however, is
defining the donut. Confusion came early. In my childhood
favorite "The Legend of Sleepy Hollow," published in 1819,
Washington Irving writes of Ichabod Crane, a schoolmaster
who has come to the home of Baltus Van Tassel to woo his
daughter Katrina. Instead, Crane is swept away by the bounty
of the Van Tassel table:

Fain would I pause to dwell upon the world of charms that burst upon the enraptured gaze of my hero as he entered the state parlor of the Van Tassel's mansion. Not those of the bevy of buxom lasses, with their luxurious display of red and white, but the ample charms of a genuine Dutch country tea table, in the sumptuous time of Autumn. Such heaped-up platters of cakes of various and almost indescribable kinds, known only to experienced Dutch housewives! There was the doughty doughnut, the tender oly koeck, and the crisp and crumbling cruller . . .

The nomenclature confounds. In modern vernacular, crullers are usually an eggy subset of donuts and *olykoek*s are linguistically vestigial, not to mention daffy. Want to sort it out? Try the word game approach: All donuts are fried doughs, but not all fried doughs are donuts. It's an accurate statement, but where does it get you? It gets you the same place you arrived in fifth grade when you plotted the trajectory of two trains, *one traveling at a rate of 33 miles per hour, and a second, moving in the opposite direction, traveling at a rate of 47 miles per hour.*

Batter is a simple delineation. For my purposes, donuts are fried batter breads of sweet, not savory, persuasion. Crullers, jumbles, bismarcks, and Berliners alike may claim origins elsewhere, but they have, over time, come to be considered as kinds of donuts by Americans.

Even a prideful Dutchman might sign off on that one. But he would hasten to point out that Irving was not alone in his advocacy of Dutch import. Others, including the aforementioned Barnard, tell the apocryphal tale of a Dutchman living in New York (né New Amsterdam) by the name of Augustus Krol, a church elder and city father who was the inspiration for the coinage of "cruller."

Serious scholars like Peter Rose, editor of *The Sensible Cook: Dutch Foodways in the Old and the New World,* see the donut—along with coleslaw, the cookie, Santa Claus, and caucus politics—as a vestige of New Netherland, the North American colony launched from the 1609 exploration of North American waterways by the Dutch East India Company. They can plot the history of the donut, back to the Dutch *olykoek* of the seventeenth century, and forward again to the modern-day *oliebolle,* still relished by the Dutch as a New Year's treat.

But scholarship rarely trumps folklore, showcased in the tale of a lady named Joralemon, described in historical accounts as a "genuine *vrouw.*" That translates as "Dutch housewife." She is said to have opened Manhattan's first donut shop in 1796, selling *olykoek*s and coffee in the financial district between Broadway and Maiden Lane. Evidently, she was a woman of no small girth, weighing in at more than two hundred pounds. When she walked the streets, hoi polloi supposedly cried, "There goes the big dough nut!"

*Olykoek*s

Adapted from The Sensible Cook *(1683), as translated and interpreted by Peter Rose in 1989, this recipe is rich but not, as the name implies, oily. If pressed to describe the taste, I would liken them to orbs of deep-fried fruitcake. And I would shout down anyone who dared dispute the goodness inherent in oil-singed orbs of fruitcake.*

- ½ cup large raisins
- 2 cups all-purpose flour
- 1 teaspoon ground cinnamon
- ½ teaspoon ground ginger
- 2 whole cloves, crushed (or ⅛ teaspoon ground cloves)
- 1 teaspoon active dry yeast
- 1 large apple, peeled and diced fine
- ¼ cup blanched almonds, crushed with the heel of a skillet
- 1 cup whole milk
- 4 tablespoons unsalted butter
- ½ gallon rapeseed or canola oil for frying
- Brown sugar for sprinkling

(continued)

Soak the raisins in a bowl filled with warm water for 30 minutes. In a large mixing bowl, combine the flour, cinnamon, ginger, cloves, and yeast.

In a medium bowl, combine the apple, almonds, and drained raisins. Heat the milk in a small saucepan over low heat until it is warm to the touch. Cut the butter into pats and add it to the milk, stirring until the butter melts. Add the milk mixture to the dry ingredients and stir until the batter forms a thick and tacky paste. Add the apple mixture and stir to incorporate the ingredients.

Pour the oil into a cast-iron Dutch oven or other deep, heavy-bottomed pot until it reaches a depth of 4 inches. Heat the oil over medium-high heat to 360°F. Form footballs of dough using two spoons, sliding each football into the oil as you go. Fry each *olykoek* for 3 to 4 minutes or until golden on both sides. Remove with a slotted spoon. Drain on wire racks and sprinkle with brown sugar while still hot. *Makes 15 to 20 olykoeks*

Say It Isn't Dough

Y ou will no doubt note that, unless I am quoting a source or summoning a particular time, I use "donut," the more modern spelling. I do so because the American donut is a modern food. By way of war and commerce, it has come to be a product of industrial throughput. And along the way, we have, to a certain extent, streamlined and standardized the words we use and the spelling we choose.

The names of yore do have their appeal. Who could resist "wonders," as donuts were billed in the *Plimouth Cookbook*? Or "dumfunnys"? And there's an honesty to using terms like "boil cakes" in Connecticut and "fat cakes" in Pennsylvania. And yes, "doughnuts" (né "dough nuts") is elucidative in a way that the shorthand coinage, "donuts," will never be.

But the slope was already slippery long before I arrived on the scene. From around 1825, the date "dough nuts" began to appear with regularity in cookbooks, less than fifty years passed before "doughnuts" became the accepted spelling. "Donuts" came to the fore in the 1920s, when the New York–based Doughnut Machine Corporation set its eyes upon foreign markets.

"In order to obviate difficulty in pronouncing 'doughnuts' in foreign languages," a press release announced, we have "been introducing the word 'donuts.'" An accompanying photograph from May 1930 shows beignet stands in France heralding *"exquis 'donuts.'"*

TWO

A Baptism in Roiling Oil

i n the spring of 2005, Kroger stores in much of the Midwest and South began selling boxes of Salvation Army donuts. They joined grocers in the Pacific Northwest and southern California who first stocked the donuts that previous winter. Packaging blazoned with the organization's red shield and featuring a comely Salvation Army maiden with a plateful of treats proclaimed the boxes "famous doughnuts." Press releases announced that these donuts were the "first and only cause-marketing product bearing the Salvation Army brand."

I didn't get the fuss. I knew the Salvation Army as a gang of kindly whitebread Protestants who dressed in grand bellhop regalia and stood in front of Kmarts at Christmastime, soliciting spare change, tooting their Seussian horns, dispensing guilt to every passerby. I didn't recall seeing donuts in their grasps. Perhaps I should have paid closer attention. Maybe they cooked their donuts in those kettles.

Not long after the Kroger debut, I brought a box home. I was hungry, and the purchase came with a promise. According to the small type, "Each time a box of Famous Doughnuts is sold, the Salvation Army's financial ammunition against hopelessness, homelessness, and hunger is replenished."

I ate one and thought, *No big deal, a cake donut with a hint of cinnamon, a trace of nutmeg.* No telling who made it, or, judging by the cocktail of chemicals contained within each fried round, where and when it was made. I tossed the rest, stowed the box on my bookshelf alongside other relics like my handheld Ron Popeil donut maker, and headed out in search of the next great eat.

three days later, back at my desk, I come upon a bit of ephemera I had found and filed and then all but forgot: a sheath of sheet music with a red, white, and blue starburst background and a bob-haired young woman at center, holding in her outstretched arms a washtub full of donuts. Among the noteworthy couplets from "My Doughnut Girl," a tribute to the Salvation Army's World War I service, are these: "But of all the folks that got mixed up / In that beastly bloody swirl / I cannot forget the graces / Of the little Doughnut Girl."

I soon learn that Elmore Leffingwell, house publicist for

the Salvation Army, cowrote the lyrics. And I marvel at his ability to manipulate the press of the day.

Later that morning, I come across a second song. Published in a July 1918 edition of the *American War Cry*, the magazine of the Salvation Army, it sets the pivotal action in France and all but promises salvation by way of fried dough:

> *A doughnut's just a doughnut, boys, 'til you are "over there,"*
> *And day and night you're in a trench away in France some-*
> *   where;*
> *You get a fresh-made doughnut, seems it comes from heaven*
> *   above,*
> *That doughnut, boys, reminds you of a slice of mother's love.*
>
> *A doughnut's just a doughnut, boys, when times of peace*
> *   prevail,*
> *But in the midst of worse than Hell where Devil's powers*
> *   assail,*
> *Where rage and hate and murder strike their hellish deadly*
> *   blows,*
> *The doughnut's a sweet-scented wreath which in God's heaven*
> *   grows.*

I beat a path to the library. And on one of the first genuinely vibrant spring days of the year, I settle onto my front porch swing with five histories of the Salvation Army, and a World War II–era novel entitled *Doughnut Dollies,* and a pitcher of gin and tonic.

Two hours pass. As the heat rises and the pitcher empties, I come to a tentative understanding of the Salvation Army role in France. Their efforts were simple and sublime: In the fall of 1917, the Salvation Army dispatched crews of men and women to tend to American troops in France. Commander Evangeline Booth expected *her* troops to comport themselves in a Christian manner, and she chose women of unimpeachable character and staunch work ethics who would be "neither tourists nor butterflies." Their mission was more secular than holy. Their charge was to minister to the homesick, to make a home away from home.

At first the Salvation Army floundered. Compared to the ten-thousand-strong YMCA force, they were understaffed. (At no time during the war would the number of American Salvation Army troops top 250.) The Lassies, as the women were known, darned socks and patched uniforms; they played Victrolas and hosted sing-alongs. The men erected canteen huts adjacent to encampments and aided soldiers sending money back home.

And then, in France in September of 1917 a sortie of four Lassies, led by a Salvation Army colonel, came upon the camp of the 1st Ammunition Train, 1st Division. They held a brief service for the men and cranked the Victrola. They handed out chocolate bars and writing tablets. The boys clamored for more. They wanted a taste of home; they wanted pie. But there was no bake oven to be had. Soon, Ensign Margaret Sheldon and Adjutant Helen Purviance hit upon a solution.

Though contemporary accounts differ as to how and why, there is no doubt that their decision to fry donuts would transform fried dough from a vaguely foreign food, loosely associated with the Dutch, into a symbol of American home and hearth, a gustatory manifestation of the ideals for which the soldiers fought. That first day, the two Lassies fried just 150 or so donuts. But as word of their loaves-and-fishes miracle spread, other Lassies took up the cause.

Working with dough made from excess rations, they employed wine bottles and shell casings as rolling pins. They cut rounds and holes with, among other devices, a jerry-rigged plunger made by fixing a camphor ice tube inside a condensed milk can and mounting the contraption on a wooden block. One account has Lassies frying the first batches in a galvanized trash can; another says it was a soldier's helmet. No matter the variation in the telling of the tale, there can be no doubt that in a very short time donuts became central to the Salvation Army ministry.

In a letter home, Purviance sketches a day in the life: "At 8 we commence to serve cocoa and coffee and make pies and doughnuts, cup cakes and fry eggs and make all kinds of eats until it is all you can see. Well can you think of two women cooking in one day 2,500 doughnuts, eight dozen cup cakes, fifty pies, 800 pan cakes and 225 gallons of cocoa, and one other girl serving it. That is a day's work in my last hut. Then meeting at night, and it lasts for two hours."

———

i bet Purviance could have used a stiff drink, say a gin and tonic, right about then. But indulgence in such blasphemous activity would have queered the paradigm. The Salvation Army relied upon stalwarts of the movement like Purviance as exemplars of Christian asceticism, founts of good newspaper copy.

And the strategy worked. The songs that captured my imagination were but small measures of the fame won by the Lassies, for the donut ministry proved a public relations coup. Leffingwell and his compatriots made the most of the opportunity, placing barely disguised advertorials in the better magazines of the day and feeding copy to a willing *New York Times.*

A Salvation Army belle in a khaki uniform and a tin helmet graced a war-era cover of *Cosmopolitan.* Lassies got star treatment in movies like *Salvation Nell, Hell's Oasis,* and *Fires of Faith.* In the latter, donuts figured large, so large that one reviewer called the melodrama a "dramatization of the doughnut," and interpreted the fires as not so much literal flames as "the spirit and courage and service" that enabled the Salvation Army to fry its way "into the hearts of the people."

When American soldiers got home from World War I, they arrived with a taste for, among other goods, French wine and filterless cigarettes. But no acquisition would affect the way Americans ate as would their taste for donuts. Indeed, so many soldiers planned to open donut shops that the military commissioned a how-to booklet for the recently furloughed.

As the war effort came to a close, the Salvation Army re-focused its efforts upon poverty eradication. But it did not desert the donut. Sorting through my files, a December 1930 edition of *Doughnut Magazine* catches my eye: A photograph shows Upper East Side matrons parading back and forth on Wall Street, dressed in high heels, draped in pearls. In their left hands they carry tambourines, the accepted conveyance for cash donations to the Salvation Army; in their right hands are rods ringed with circles of fried dough, which, on the day in question, fetched the nosebleed price of a dollar.

Lassie Loops

This recipe was inspired by instructions that Stella Young, the Salvation Army pinup girl of World War I, dictated to Sally Levitt Steinberg when the author of The Donut Book *visited Young at her home in Old Orchard Beach, Maine. During their interview Young let slip to Steinberg that, owing to primitive battlefield conditions, the donuts the Lassies fried during the war were not marvels of the pastry arts. These, on the other hand, prove true Commander Evangeline Booth's billing of the Salvation Army's way with the "winsome, attractive coquetries of the round, brown doughnut."*

- 6 cups all-purpose flour
- 2 cups plus 2 tablespoons sugar
- ½ teaspoon salt
- 4 teaspoons baking powder
- 1 tablespoon lard or shortening
- 2 large eggs
- 1½ cups whole milk
- ½ gallon vegetable oil for frying
- 1 teaspoon ground cinnamon

In a large mixing bowl, combine the flour, 2 cups of the sugar, the salt, and baking powder. Rub in the lard or shortening with your fingertips until the mixture is pebbly. Set aside.

In a medium bowl, beat the eggs well, then beat in the milk. Set aside. Working either directly on your flour board, or in a shallow pan or bowl, create a well in the center of the flour mixture. Pour the egg-milk mixture into the well and start working the dry ingredients into the wet, using a pastry scraper or your hands to gently fold the dry and wet ingredients together. Be careful not to knead the dough like bread; work it gently to avoid creating a chewy texture. Turn the resulting mound over a couple of times on a lightly floured surface and roll out with a rolling pin to ¼-inch thickness.

Pour the oil into a cast-iron Dutch oven or other

(continued)

deep, heavy-bottomed pot until it reaches a depth of
3 or 4 inches. Heat the oil over medium-high heat to
325°F. Using a dough cutter, cut the dough into rounds,
then cut out a smaller round from each for the center.
Gather the scraps and reroll the dough as necessary. Fry
each loop for two minutes per side or until puffed and
golden. Remove with a slotted spoon and drain on wire
racks. Toss the cinnamon and remaining 2 tablespoons
sugar together in a large brown paper bag. While the
donuts are still warm, add a few at a time, shaking to
cover with the cinnamon sugar. *Makes about 24 loops*

Glazed and Confused

When I grow weary digging through newspaper
morgues, trying to make sense of America's love affair with donuts, I turn to music. Queuing old 45s, I learn that
the Salvation Army was not the only group inspired to marry
popping grease and clashing cymbals.

First the profane: The Willis Brothers, on their 1969 album *Hey, Mister Truck Driver,* cut "The Only Shoulder (A
Trucker Can Cry On)," "White Lines and Roadside Signs,"
and "Diesel Drivin' Donut Dunkin' Dan." In 1972, the Mills

Brothers cut "Pull the Shade, Mrs. Slade," "We're All Losers
('Til We Find Love)," and "A Donut and a Dream" for the album of the same title.

Maria Muldaur of "Midnight at the Oasis" fame cut an al-
bum in 1974 titled *Waitress in the Donut Shop,* which featured
the song "It Ain't the Meat, It's the Motion." Spark Plug
Smith and Tallahassee Tight, on their 1995 album, cut
"Stopped Clock Blues," "Motherless Boy," and "Mama's
Doughnut." In 1997, the Last Chance Jug Band cut "Who
Pumped the Wind in My Doughnut?" And in 2003, Bag of
Donuts, an art rock ensemble from New Orleans, laid down
the classic anthem "Glazed and Confused."

And now the sacred: Carl Sandburg, Pulitzer Prize–
winning poet and champion of free verse, once recorded an
album, *Flat Rock Ballads.* Included were the ditties "Suckin'
Cider Through a Straw" and "The Doughnut Man." Roly-poly
Burl Ives cut a selection of children's tunes, including "Lolli-
pop Tree," "Sow Took the Measles," and "Donut Song." And
in December of 1962—the month and year of my birth—jazz
master Ornette Coleman, in concert at Town Hall in New
York City, cut a nine-minute ode to the donut—and a four-
minute ode to sadness.

THREE

Man and Machine

most people come to Seattle's Pike Place Market to watch fishmongers throw salmon from ice bins to cash registers. Not this tourist. The double-helix tosses fail to hold my attention. Catch a twelve-pounder behind your back and see if I care. I'm drawn by music that is primal and insistent. I'm drawn by the smells of frying dough and cinnamon.

Jason Cread, the one-man band who works the Daily Dozen Donuts stand, keeps his black hair long and spiky. When he bops his head to the sounds of a favorite band—say local faves Hellshock or the irrepressible Dead Kennedys— his hair shades his eyes from the bright lights above. Jason wears a studded dog collar around his neck and longer amulet-style studded collars on each wrist. His boom box, from which various screeches and thumps emanate, sports a KEEP MUSIC EVIL bumper sticker.

I assume he's a musician, but Jason says, "Nah, I got a drum kit, but I don't know what to do with it. Right now, I'm a donut guy." As we talk, Jason whacks out a rhythm with a pair of metal tongs, snatching donuts from a glazing carousel connected to a conveyor belt cooker. Customers come and go. He makes change, offering each person a sheepish smile. Between pulls on an espresso machine, Jason pops white paper bags open for each order of donuts, snapping his wrist downward, listening for the satisfying, percussive *thwop*.

He likes that thwop. With each thwop, he smiles. And when the sound of the espresso machine gets too nasal, too angular to hear the thwop, he cranks the bass on the boom box and spins the volume dial, digging deeper for a rhythm, any rhythm, to ride for the next fifteen minutes until his shift is over.

Jason works a Donut Robot Mark II. The machine is an engineering marvel, a countertop workhorse fitted, in a lateral layout, with a ring-plunger at one end, a conveyor belt chamber of burbling oil in the center, and, at the finish, the aforementioned glazing carousel plush with jimmies and crushed peanuts.

Absent Jason's obvious talent, the machine would still

draw a crowd, fascinated by the sheer Rube Goldberg genius of a device dedicated to the constant turnout of miniature cake donuts. But for a student of donut lore, the machine offers more. It offers entrée to an era when donuts and a myriad of other foodstuffs from sliced white bread to breakfast cereal were first produced and—in the case of meals eaten at the nation's flourishing automats—delivered to consumers by contraptions instead of human hands. "Every day [it] seems some ingenious new wrinkle is devised to lessen labor," observed a *Ladies' Home Journal* columnist in 1928.

adolph Levitt is considered the inventor of the Wonderful Almost Human Automatic Doughnut Machine. More so than John Blondell of Thomaston, Maine, the man who in 1872 requested patent on a spring-loaded donut cutter, or Frank Morris of Philadelphia, who in 1919 filed for patent on a machine designed to cook "the ordinary cruller or the doughnut of annular form," Levitt is recognized as the man who liberated fried dough from the tedium of labor.

It helped that Levitt was a bold and keen-minded promoter who understood the kid-in-a-candy-store fascination of watching donuts roll by on an assembly line. Writing in *The New Yorker*, James Thurber described Levitt's machine as "cleaner than a steam shovel in an excavation," whatever the heck that means. "Doughnuts float dreamily through a grease canal in a glass-enclosed machine," wrote Thurber, "walk dreamily up a moving ramp, and tumble dreamily into an outgoing basket."

According to Thurber, a Mr. Sugarman claimed that Levitt's company, the Doughnut Machine Corporation of America, removed "the doughnut from the mire of prejudice that surrounded the heavy, grease-soaked product of the old oaken bucket and made it into a light, puffy product of a machine." To be sure, the stigma was there. Much of the market for donuts was born of World War I Salvation Army work, when the Lassies cooked donuts in sometimes squalid battlefield settings. Levitt and company guessed correctly that back home veterans would seek better, more modern conditions.

But Levitt was not alone. In 1920, soon after he debuted his first machine in a Harlem, New York, bakery, the Square Donut Company of America, a Washington, D.C.–based concern, began selling stock and promoting Donos, square donuts, as well as patented machines that produced "square donuts faster and more economically than doughnuts were ever manufactured before."

belshaw Brothers, founded in Seattle in 1923 and now the manufacturer of my friend Jason's Donut Robot Mark II, also embraced the machine ideal. They called their first product the Sanitary Doughnut Machine and staked their reputation on doughnuts "untouched by human hands."

Belshaw Brothers is the sole survivor of the early automated donut era, when Dono and the Donut Corporation of America ruled. It was their story that lured me to Seattle in the first place, their product that beckoned me to the fish-mongers. Belshaw Brothers has endured market crests and valleys; their products have cranked out donuts to the tune of Bing Crosby, Tiny Tim—and Hellshock too.

Today their tabletop models are fixtures of market she-bangs like Daily Dozen as well as aircraft carriers like the USS *Enterprise*. Their wares are such a part of our national fabric that they have become part and parcel of the American incarceration experience: prisons from San Quentin, Cali-fornia, to Atlanta, Georgia, stock their machines, though, ac-cording to Mike Baxter, Belshaw's marketing ace, "they use a special prison package machine, one that can't be easily dis-assembled to make shivs."

After a tour of the Belshaw plant with Baxter at my side—ogling new Century 600 machines capable of five hundred dozen donuts per hour, inspecting aluminum cruller dies they call Frenchies—I return the next day to Pike Place and to the Daily Dozen. Jason Cread is again at the helm.

I try to tell him of the proud legacy he has inherited, if only for the duration of his employ. I tell him that an under-standing of the American donut requires the resolution of unique tensions between tradition and modernity, between the valorization of handcrafted and machine-made goods. I tell him that of America's foremost folks foods—fried chicken, hamburgers, and apple pie included—donuts were the first to arrive on the nation's palate by way of an ongo-ing fascination with labor-saving devices and a spiraling obsession with cleanliness. I tell him that the machine he now operates, the one he's banging like a set of cymbals, is an instrument of modernity, an American icon. When I've finished my speechifying, Jason looks up through a tangle of hair, pops a bag, and asks me how many donuts I want. I tell him a half-dozen, with powdered sugar. Jason turns to snag my order and resumes a conversation with a friend. "Yeah, man, I'm engaged," he says. "I love her. But I'm pretty sure whatever we do for a wedding won't be legal. We're talking about having a goat sacrifice at the ceremony."

Lazy Man's Ersatz Donuts

Pushing the labor-saving impulse to its most absurd conclusion, I offer this cheater's path to fried delight. Sure, it's a goof, but the donuts cook up light and fluffy. (I keep a can of Pillsbury's best secreted in the back of our fridge for those mornings when my son, Jess, clamors for a homemade donut but I can't rationalize the mile-long trek to the store for eggs.) And I defy you to declaim the chemical compounds within a cylinder of grocery store biscuit dough as being any more objectionable than the extenders and such present in the typical commercial donut mix.

(continued)

■ ½ gallon peanut or vegetable oil for frying
■ 1 10-pack cylinder canned biscuit dough
■ 1 tablespoon ground cinnamon
■ ¼ cup sugar

Pour the oil into a cast-iron Dutch oven or other deep, heavy-bottomed pot, until it reaches a depth of at least 2 but not more than 3 inches. Heat the oil over medium-high heat to 375°F. Extract the biscuits from the can and pat the circles of dough out to 1½ times their original diameter, or about ¼ inch thick.

Cut out donut holes using a bottle cap or a shot glass. Slip the rings into the oil, working in two batches. Do not crowd the pot. Cook for a minute or two per side, flipping the donuts with care to prevent splatter. When light golden brown on both sides, use a slotted spoon to remove the donuts from the pan to a wire rack and fry the holes. Using a metal slotted spoon or spatula keeps the holes moving, as they can become weighted and difficult to flip. Drain the holes on a wire rack.

Mix the cinnamon and sugar together in a large

brown paper bag and drop the donuts in one at a time, shaking lightly to distribute evenly.

Add the holes all at once, shaking in the same fashion. *Makes about 12 donuts*

Homer Price Gets Looped

i could tell you that my fascination with donut machines was born of companies like Belshaw and their machines. But the truth is, I came to know these machines by way of a children's book, *Homer Price*. Written and illustrated by Robert McCloskey of *Make Way for Ducklings* fame, the 1943 book sketches the misadventures of a boy of ten or twelve.

Chapter three, my favorite, tells of the afternoon Homer spends at his Uncle Ulysses' lunch room in the vaguely mid-western town of Centerburg. Left in charge of his uncle's new donut machine, Homer manages to befriend a hobo, learn a secret recipe from a mink coat–clad heiress, and find a lost diamond bracelet.

All the while, his uncle's machine has gone haywire, and "rings of batter kept right on dropping into the hot fat, and the automatic gadget kept turning them over, and the other automatic gadget kept right on giving them a little push, and the doughnuts kept right on rolling down the little chute just as regular as a clock can tick—they just kept right on a comin', an' a comin', an' a comin', and a' comin'."

The scene was, for a boy yet to eat his fill of donuts, a preview of glories yet to come.

FOUR

A Trapeze,
a Parachute,
a Donut

One of the first things I did while researching this book was spend a day in the reading room of the New York Public Library. It's a gorgeous space, a church of learning. And as far as I can tell, it's the library with the most complete collection of *Doughnut Magazine* back issues.

As the leading manufacturer of mixes and the machines that cooked them, the Doughnut Corporation of America took a proprietary interest in the good name of cake donuts. And *Doughnut Magazine* served as the disseminator of *good news* regarding fried dough. But donut advocacy required vigilance.

Some of the most pernicious attacks on donuts were perpetrated by dietmongers, people, and institutions the magazine damned as "food faddists." In a March/April 1935 issue,

Doughnut Magazine reminded readers that John Harvey Kellogg had "doomed the race of man unless it took up an exclusive milk and vegetable diet." And it warned of threats such as the "groundless defamation of white bread." But the best defense, then as now, proved to be a good offense.

In 1941, at a time when many people were dismissing donuts as leaden calorie bombs, the company introduced Dr. J. Howard Crum's Famous Donut Reducing Diet. Crum, who appeared in advertisements of the day wearing a stethoscope and looking suspect, endorsed the plan as a "sensible, pleasant way to take off pounds." The diet, he said, was "easy to stay on, because good donuts supply your daily need for energy."

Just a few years previous, Kern's Cake Donuts of Stockton, California, had published a booklet proclaiming that the need for energy was top-of-mind: "The Pilgrim Mothers recognized the energy stored up in doughnuts and served them three times a day, so that their men folks might better withstand the hardships of those early days."

Beneath was a chart, headed by the following rhetorical: "Did you know that there is more food value in doughnuts than in most of the foods you eat every day?" Of course, these were the days when calories were referred to as energy units, and a measure of 2,040 calories per pound for doughnuts was considered not a threat to the midsection but a boon, especially in light of the meager energy stores in 1,555-calories-per-pound pork chops and 1,885-calories-per-pound cheese.

———

e ven today, while their stock price no longer soars, the opening of a Krispy Kreme franchise still draws pajama-clad fanatics willing to stand in line through the night to be first through the doors after a daybreak ribbon cutting. Documenting the scene with a mike in one hand and an original glazed in the other, "Live at Five" local news crews still feed the fervor, broadcasting the circus, extending the citizenry's glazed and amused honeymoon for the better part of a year.

Yet Krispy Kreme, for all its savvy, can't match the inventiveness of America's disparate donut shop operators. Nor, in its time, could the Doughnut Corporation of America. In the manner of nineteenth-century snake oil salesmen peddling herbed alcohol concoctions as medicinal panaceas, donut shop owners have long sold deep-fried rings of dough as more than a sum of ingredients.

Patriotism played a role. In the wake of World War I, United Press declared, "The doughnut—once a mere culinary zero—has returned from the war improved in health and grown in popularity. Salvation Army Lassies who dealt out the circlets while the Hun dealt out shrapnel are credited with popularizing the 'sinker.'"

The donut has proven best suited, however, to the grand stunt, the headline-grabbing goof. As in the time a midget on a flying trapeze dodged the electrical lines, cleared the roof of the drive-thru shop below, and flew through the center of the oversized icon mounted atop Randy's Donuts of Los Angeles. As in the time a Redfield, South Dakota, bakery owner named George Hopkins hired a biplane to circle his hometown and floated donut-filled sample bags fitted with tissue-paper parachutes to his fellow citizens. As in the time stuntman Shipwreck Kelly stood on his head, on the lip of a New Yorker skyscraper, and dunked thirteen cake donuts into a cup of coffee while throngs of onlookers craned their necks upward to see his feet kick, his arms windmill.

Integral to each of these stunts is the donut's flyweight cultural status, the acceptance on the part of cooks as well as consumers that the donut is not so much focus as foil. Sail a midget through its center and the donut is transformed. Set it adrift on a tissue parachute and the donut achieves currency. Eat it with aplomb and the donut matters.

Donut recipes and plating schemes play a role too. The topological simplicity of the form lends itself to rococo riffs. Donut promoters of yore understood this, back when they were up-selling Americans on the virtues of pineapple donut sandwiches made with laterally bisected cake donuts and slices of Dole's best, not to mention donut snowballs, topped with whipped cream, shredded coconut, and maraschino cherries.

Another yield from the geek trove: In 1952, the *New York Times* reported the debut of the pretzel donut, a "revolutionary innovation," as well as "other odd ways of using doughnuts," including a "doughnut salad with dates, bananas, oranges, and watercress." Three days later, a letter to the editor appeared in the *Times* suggesting that "all true lovers of the royal doughnut must band together and form a united front against the intrusion of such indigestibles." The writer, Gilbert Doane of Madison, Wisconsin, proclaimed, "We need a Society for the Protection of the Doughnut."

Doane's notion never took flight. If such a society had come into being, would their sons and daughters have stood idly by when, in 2004, proprietors of Mulligan's, a sports bar in suburban Atlanta, rolled out the Luther Burger, a bacon cheeseburger served between top and bottom "buns" made from Krispy Kreme donuts? Wouldn't they have condemned the fusillade of press—the *Chicago Tribune,* the *Los Angeles Times*—that reported the rollout?

And what might the inheritors of Doane's plaint have done in response to the 2003 opening of Voodoo Doughnut and Wedding Chapel in Portland, Oregon? Would they have thrown a collective hissy fit and hacked up Voodoo's fry kettles, secure in the knowledge that any donut shop that opens at ten in the evening and serves such aberrances as Grape Apes (raised donuts iced with vanilla and sprinkled with powdered grape drink mix) and Dirty Snowballs (chocolate cake donuts filled with cream and slathered with pink marshmallow frosting) is worthy of a Carrie Nation, chop-'em-to-pieces rejoinder?

To donut purists, such a response might seem altogether warranted. But for the press, the real story of their first year in business was the hasty removal of the infamous NyQuil and Pepto-Bismol donuts from the Voodoo Doughnuts roster.

That story burned bright for a while. And then, in early 2005, just when the NyQuil buzz was ebbing, I caught wind of the next development.

According to an article in *The Christian Science Monitor*, Voodoo Doughnuts has taken to hosting free Monday-night Swahili language lessons. The instructor, Abdi Muhina, teaches his students to "translate songs like 'Don't Worry, Be Happy' from English to Swahili and to play 'Swahopoly' [Swahiliized Monopoly]." Liz Nakazawa, the *Christian Science Monitor* reporter, makes no mention of product tie-ins. But how far behind can they be?

Voodoo Dirt Donuts

The boys and girls in Portland use yeast-raised donuts as their base. But I think a cake donut holds up better to the burden of Oreo topsoil. I borrow the cake donut here from Zingerman's Roadhouse in Ann Arbor, Michigan. It's the same cake donut highlighted in the coda chapter of this book. The glaze, however, is a full frontal homage to Voodoo. Be sure to make it at the last minute, or your dirt will go soggy.

ZINGERMAN'S ROADHOUSE DONUTS
   ■ 1 recipe Zingerman's Roadhouse Donuts
   (page 164)

DIRT GLAZE
   ■ ¾ cup confectioners' sugar
   ■ 2 tablespoons whole milk
   ■ 1 teaspoon vanilla extract
   ■ 12 Oreo cookies

In a medium bowl, mix the milk with the confectioners' sugar, stirring to make a thin paste. Add the vanilla and stir again. Crumble the cookies into the glaze, working to achieve Oreo particles of a size similar to what you would find in a Dairy Queen Blizzard. Trowel the mixture on the donuts and set aside for 15 minutes or so, until the glaze begins to set.

The Hole Truth

i n November of 1941, in the waning days before the Japanese attack upon Pearl Harbor thrust the United States into World War II, a panel assembled at the Astor Hotel in New York City. The mood was gay. Three celebrity judges—literary whiz Clifton Fadiman, actor Franklin Adams, and actress Elsa Maxwell—presided with tongues planted firmly in cheek and pyramids of donuts within easy reach.

Seated on a dais in a chandelier-lit ballroom, they entertained arguments from two jurists charged with resolving—once, and for all time—who was responsible for the hole in the donut. Defending the claim of Hanson Crockett Gregory, a ship's captain from the village of Clam Cove, Maine, was his second cousin, Fred Crockett. In opposition was Henry Ellis, an attorney from Cape Cod, Massachusetts, who pledged to weave a tale of Native American birth.

The press reported the event as if it were a news story and adopted the suggested sobriquet "The Great Donut Debate." Never mind that, owing to the nationalistic fervor sweeping the country, the odds were stacked against Ellis. Or that no one involved took the debate too seriously. Or that the Doughnut Corporation of America likely paid claimants and jurors alike for their appearances. Never mind any of that. The debate, like the stories told throughout the years, made good copy. And in those anxious times, good copy was a godsend.

e llis argued that Americans owed the donut hole to the archery skill of a brave who, upon launching an arrow through the window of a log cabin, did not pierce his intended victim, a Pilgrim woman, but the fry cake she was pulling from a skillet. The story was inventive, and only a bit less plausible than any other that would be told that evening. But Ellis provided no supporting evidence, while Crockett flashed sheaths of documents.

Crockett had an arsenal of stories to call upon. He could sketch Gregory as a child prodigy of fifteen, the youngest captain in the Maine fleet. Aboard the ship *Frypan*, while munching a fried cake, Gregory was thrown to the deck by a swell. Upon clambering to his feet, he impaled his fry cake on the ship's wheel to save the goodie for later, wrested control of the boat, and—in that very moment—resolved that all future fried cakes would have such a hole for ease of stowage in rough seas.

Or Crockett could play the safety angle. He could add a moral dimension, a lesson learned at sea. Same swell, same captain. Only this time Gregory loses six men overboard. Some versions blame a fierce squall, others a recent meal of leaden fry cakes that made the men sink like plummets. In either iteration, Gregory finds inspiration in the life preservers that could have saved his men, and soon begins punching holes in fry cakes with a shipboard belaying pin.

And there was always the tale of Gregory, the seafaring inventor. That was a good one. In a turn-of-the-twentieth-century interview, published by *The Boston Globe* and unearthed by donut historian Sally Levitt Steinberg, the man himself told of his time aboard the schooner *Isaach Achorn*, engaged in the lime trade. The year, as is customary, was 1847, and Gregory was suffering from indigestion after eating a mess of "greasy sinkers."

He thought to himself, "Why wouldn't a space inside solve the difficulty?" Suddenly, "I took the cover off the ship's tin pepper box, and—I cut into the middle of that doughnut the first hole ever seen by mortal eyes." Slightly embarrassed, he added, "Of course, a hole ain't so much, but it's the best part of the doughnut—you'd think so if you had ever tasted the doughnuts we used to eat." Toward the close of the interview, the *Globe* reporter asked Gregory if he was pleased with his invention. Gregory said, "Was Columbus pleased?"

In the end, Fred Crockett went with the simplest of stories. And the judges ruled in his favor, declaring that in 1847 Hanson Crockett Gregory "was in the kitchen of his home watching his mother make fried cakes. He asked her why the centers were so soggy. She said that for some reason they never got cooked. Then the boy decided to poke out the center of the uncooked cakes with a fork. His mother cooked them. They were the first [ring] donuts."

Six years later, friends of the Gregory family installed a bronze tablet at the cornerstone of his boyhood home. They made no reference to how or why he poked the first hole. They did not set the action on land or at sea. They merely inscribed these words: "This is the birthplace of Captain Hanson Gregory who first invented the hole in the donut in the year 1847."

In 2002, Candy Sagon, a reporter for *The Washington Post,* tracked down Fred Crockett at his home in Rockport, Maine. He was, by then, ninety-one. But he was still spry, still talkative. And he still began each morning with a cup of coffee and a plain cake donut. His recollection of the Astor Hotel event was tinged with regret. "After the debate, some wealthy people offered to set me up with a donut shop, but I turned them down," he told Sagon. "Maybe I could have been a millionaire."

of eels and
donuts and
new england

i f the Dutch were the likely sires of American donuts, then New Englanders were their scions. You could make a case that New Englanders owe their zeal for fried doughs to the eleven-year sojourn the Pilgrims spent in Holland before setting sail for the New World. Or you could argue that access to oil and occupation are the true influences.

Sandy Oliver, an historian of nineteenth-century New England, is a member of the oil camp. She says that when a whaling crew filled its thousandth barrel of oil, the captain would reward the men with whale blubber–fried donuts. (Those of you who object to lard-fried donuts, take note!) In 1845, Mary Brewster, a cook aboard the whaleship *Tiger*, recorded the prospect: "At 7 p.m. boats got fast to a whale and at 9 got him to the ship. Men all singing and bawling Doughnuts Doughnuts to morrow as this will certainly make 1,000 barrels."

For whalers, donuts were a reward; they were at sea to collect oil, not expend it. Back home, where the primary ingredients—flour, sweetener, and fat—were easily accessed, donuts were comparatively humble. They were a relatively humdrum fare, more everyday bread than special-occasion dessert.

At least that's how I choose to make gastronomic sense of my discovery that, on Cape Cod in 1849, the wife of a Wellfleet oysterman served Henry David Thoreau a breakfast of eels, green beans, and donuts. It's the rationalization I use when pondering why characters in Harriet Beecher Stowe's fiction ate cheese and donuts between church services. The latter is a habit that I can't quite conjure with pleasure, even when taking into account the empirical brilliance of that New England favorite, cheese-capped apple pie.

FIVE

Prospectus for
the New England
Donut Museum

i have a donut fantasy. Doesn't every boy, every man? In my fantasy, the city of Boston operates a Museum of the New England Donut, a hippodrome of fried dough designed by Frank Gehry. Beyond a general charge that the museum valorizes the form, I'll leave the look of the temple to Gehry's team of imagineers. After working with Disney on that kinetic Los Angeles concert hall, they should know the drill: playfully referential but functional.

My fantasy has myriad sources. Foremost is the notion, confirmed by time on the road, that when it comes to donuts New England is a place apart. There are a number of ways to argue this point, but I'm fond of sketching the sugar on snow ritual, an only-in-New-England feed. Here's how traditionalists do it:

In the early spring, when snow still blankets the ground and the maple sap begins to flow, you tromp into the woods and tap a maple tree. And then another and another, collecting the sap in a kettle. Back at camp, someone builds a roaring fire. Once you have enough sap to fill a kettle, you return to camp, set your kettle over the fire, and boil the sap down until it approximates syrup.

Meanwhile, you fill another kettle with oil, mix a batch of dough, and begin frying donuts. Then you pull a jar of sour pickles from your knapsack, set them in the snow to cool, and you celebrate the first sugaring of the season by ladling syrup on the snow and peeling back strips of elastic candy. After about the third taste of maple taffy, you need a palate cleanser. The bright pucker of the pickle takes care of that. But it accomplishes the task too well, which is, of course, where the donut comes in, tipping the balance away from the sour, back toward the sweet.

my museum will feature a sugar-on-snow amphitheater, where the sap is always running and snow forever blankets the ground. But educational offerings will augment the savory exhibits. Toward that end, I see an animated diorama, something along the lines of Walt Disney World's Hall of Presidents, circa 1971.

Instead of a debate over the rights of man and dependent clauses in the Declaration of Independence, I envision a restaging of the Great Donut Debate. Visitors will witness a searing exchange of ideas and intellect during which, once and for all, the matter of who cut the first hole in a donut is decided: On the left, representing the estate of Chief High Eagle of the Wampanoag tribe of Massachusetts, stands an android Dave Barry; on the right, defending the honor of Captain Hanson Crockett Gregory of Maine, an android P. J. O'Rourke.

After the debate comes to a close, a side curtain opens, a screen unfurls, and a film rolls. I call this the *It's a Small World* documentary. We view New England citizens, recent immigrants, dressed in the garb of their homeland, cooking and eating all manner of fried doughs:

The Pilgrims come first, with *olykoeks* they acquired from the Dutch. We watch Italian immigrants docking at Providence, Rhode Island, celebrating St. Joseph's Day by building food altars and frying *zeppole*. We see a Portuguese family dock at Boston and, through the magic of time-lapse photography, we watch them acquire one, then three, then twelve Dunkin' Donut franchises, until, by some estimates, as many as 40 percent of the Dunkin' Donuts in the Boston area are Portuguese-owned.

Speaking of Dunkin' Donuts, I see them as concessionaire for the museum. In addition to opening a retail store, I envision a storyboard homage to founder William Rosenberg, beginning in 1946 with the fleet of canteen trucks from which he and his workers peddled coffee, sandwiches, and donuts to Boston factory workers. By panel two in the exhibit, the year is 1948 and Rosenberg is the proprietor of a restaurant without wheels, the Open Kettle donut shop. Two years and one panel later, he opens the first Dunkin' Donuts in suburban Quincy. And so it goes, panel by panel, success by success, until Dunkin' Donuts, the pride of New England, is ringing up sales of three billion dollars a year.

But enough with the numbers. In my museum we won't pummell the museum-goer with business statistics. Highlights from Rosenberg's personal life will provide levity. Look for the panel that details the day he met Mario Puzo, author of the *Godfather,* at a weight-loss clinic. You'll learn that Puzo had a hand in convincing Rosenberg to write a memoir, *Time to Make the Donuts.*

Of course, I'll tweak the Dunkin' Donuts schematic a bit to fit the museum's needs. Instead of a grab bag of flavor combinations concocted by a retinue of middle-aged flavor chemists intent upon snagging the adolescent market with chocolate-chipotle frosted donuts spackled with jalapeño crunch chips, my museum will use the Dunkin' Donuts commitment to fifty-two flavors as an edible organizing principle.

I got the idea for the museum, or at least the basis for the idea, from David Gravino, proprietor of Iggy's Doughboys and Chowder House, down near the beach in Warwick, Rhode Island. When I made a trek to eat his sugar-dusted pillows of fried dough, David emerged from behind the counter to talk about the universality of fritters and tell me about a late and lamented emporium in Las Vegas, a place called something like Mom's Fried Breads.

The way I remember David telling the story, the walls at

Mom's were covered with the names of fried doughs served the world over. And Mom's made every effort to serve the fried dough of any nationality or ethnicity that walked through the door. I'm thinking that this New England Donut Museum of mine will aim for the same goal.

For starters, we'll charge the chemists at Dunkin' Donuts with serving a representative sample. Sure, they'll raise a hue and cry at the start. But after a few reconnaissance missions, they'll discover that in New England the doughboys served at Iggy's taste remarkably similar to the Baptist Cakes of Connecticut (known in some circles as Holey Pokes). And before you know it, they'll be petitioning for speaking parts in the revised *It's a Small World* documentary that our barnstorming director of outreach will show to every fifth-grade class that books her.

Baptist Cakes

During the 1930s, Ida Lee Hale ran the Hartford-Hale House, a tearoom in Glastonbury, Connecticut. She served these hole-less fried cakes as a sweet accompaniment to a supper of, say, corned beef hash. By the time I try her cakes they have made their way south to Mississippi, their legacy entrusted to her great-grandson Tommy Freeland, an Oxford attorney. Tommy tells me that his family tradition has long been to dip the cakes in warm milk or maple syrup. "They were part of an evening meal in the winter," says Tommy. "We always did it that way, just like we buttered noses on birthdays, so you slid into the new year." This recipe is adapted from Tommy's.

- 1 package (2¼ teaspoons) active dry yeast
- 1½ cups water
- 1½ cups whole milk, at room temperature
- 1 tablespoon salt
- 3 tablespoons sugar
- 2 tablespoons shortening, melted and cooled slightly
- 8 to 9 cups all-purpose flour, sifted
- 2 tablespoons unsalted butter, softened
- ½ gallon peanut or vegetable oil for frying

Dissolve the yeast in ½ cup warm water, stirring. Meanwhile, in a large bowl, combine the remaining 1 cup water (cool, not warm), the milk, salt, and sugar. Add the yeast mixture and the shortening. Add the flour, stirring until the mixture is stiff. Remove the dough to a floured work surface and knead as you would bread, until a rough ball can be formed.

Grease a heatproof bowl or kettle with the softened butter. Place the dough in the bowl and cover with plastic. Store in a warm place until the dough doubles in size, about 1 hour. Roll the dough out with a rolling pin to a thickness of ½ inch, then cut into 2-inch squares. Place on a cookie sheet and cover with plastic. Set aside for 15 minutes.

Pour the oil into a cast-iron Dutch oven or other deep, heavy-bottomed pot until it reaches a depth of 3 to 4 inches. Heat the oil to 360°F. Fry each square for 1 to 2 minutes per side or until golden on both sides. Remove with a slotted spoon and drain on wire racks.

Serve with a dunking bowl of warm milk topped with a pat of butter. Or maybe a bowl of maple syrup heated until warm. *Makes 40 to 50 cakes*

Breakfast with Eleanor

the cop + donut = bliss formula is an old joke. With the exception of a recent *Late Show* spoof of David Letterman's summer vacation at the shore, complete with bathing beauties and four cops bobbing in the water begging for crullers like seals for chum, the gags are just about spent.

Of late, in a bid to maintain relevancy, donut humor has taken on a darker tone. Witness the BAD COP, NO DONUT bumper stickers that began to appear in the wake of the Rodney King riots. And then there's the film *Dirty Cop, No Donut,* a so-called shockumentary about a corrupt police officer, recently released from jail, intent on a taste of revenge and a couple dozen chocolate glazed.

The high point of donut humor may have come during World War II. As the story is told, Eleanor Roosevelt was reviewing the troops, making inquiries as to this sergeant's hometown, that private's well-being, when she came upon a crew preparing breakfast. She wondered why the cook was slapping a round of dough against his chest. "I'm making pancakes," he explained. "Isn't that a funny way to make pancakes?" Roosevelt asked. "That's nothing," he said. "You ought to see how we make doughnuts."

SIX

Deep-Fried Hyperbole

i can't think of a place I would rather be on Easter morning than standing in line at Butler's Colonial Donut House in the burg of Westport, Massachusetts, down near the shore. I have arrived early; the line is blessedly short. Among the noteworthy are a mother with two teenage boys, one of whom keeps smashing his face against the pastry case, leaving lurid, lip-shaped smudges on the pane of glass that separates him from a tray of chocolate-glazed yeast donuts; a priest from nearby Our Lady of Grace Catholic Church; and a man in brown coveralls, clutching a piece of paper, the front of which reads MANIFEST, the back of which is chicken-scratched with dozen-each orders from his coworkers.

This is my third time at the counter on this chilly morning. I started off slow. First a cinnamon sugar–dusted cake. Then a chocolate-glazed yeast. I didn't want to appear overeager. I didn't want to tip my hand to proprietor Alex Kogler. He might see me for who I am: the fiend who, for the past month, kept dialing his number, asking after the whipped cream, praying that an early spring and an attendant rise in temperature would not foil my pilgrimage in search of Butler's fabled long johns.

I had last dialed their number on Good Friday. Alex's wife, Chris, told me that although the heat was inching upward they would not impose an early moratorium on whipped cream. She told me that it was their policy to try to serve whipped cream until at least Memorial Day. Of course, she allowed, whipped cream is fragile. Humidity can kill a good cream. But at the very worst, she assured me, they would be serving long johns for another month.

All assurances aside, I was twitching when I crossed their threshold at seven and spied the tray of long johns. And I'm still twitching now, though my state might be owing to the three cups of coffee I drank on the drive down from Boston. And then there were those two primer donuts.

A long john crafted by Alex Kogler looks like a hot dog bun turned on its side. A little shorter, sure, and not quite as thick around the middle, but a hot dog bun nonetheless. I order two—one for examining, one for eating.

On my periphery, I catch sight of Chris, slitting the ingots along their sides, piping thin streams of black raspberry jelly down the center. Beyond her, I can see the clapboard home where the Koglers live when they are not selling donuts. In the foreground, a crew of three teenage girls, their pigtailed hair gathered tight in scrunchies, boxes orders and makes change. Front and center stands Alex, a former professional hockey player with the kind of forearms a steroid-popper would envy. He's working a Gatling gun–like device, popping dough blanks from molds, arranging them in fry trays.

The long john arrives on my flank from Chris's piping station by way of a fourth scrunchie-wearer, whose charge it is to stuff the long johns with snow drifts of cream. I prod one, investigating the texture. How to describe the texture? I'll give it a couple of shots: How about, *Imagine a bun, spun from cotton candy.* Or, *Imagine a bun, made not with flour and water and yeast, but flour and water and helium.*

Neither description satisfies me. But the long john does. Rich as all get-out, sprightly with berries, swaddled in dairy, it lives up to the impossible standards of my dreams. I eat the first at the cash register while rummaging through my pockets for change. The second, the one intended for textural investigation, goes down my gullet while I sit, stoop-shouldered, beneath a ceiling low enough to give pause to a Lilliputian.

Alex Kogler doesn't have time for my hyperbole. Or my leading questions about what it means to run a small donut shop. Alex doesn't consider himself a peddler of moonbeams and starshine. He's no stalwart in the struggle against big-box retail dominance. He's a craftsman, like any other. And right now he's busy whacking dough into shape on a work table.

Over the course of a couple of hours spent at one of the two stools in this cracker box of a shop, I am able to tease the story of the long johns from him. In the process, I learn a bit about the workings of a family-owned donut shop. But my gleanings are oblique.

Take product development: Alex says that the long johns became a part of the regular roster a few years after the Koglers bought the business from the Butler family. "It was back in 1982," he tells me. "Chris was in the hospital, about to have our son. I was doing a bit of experimenting in the kitchen, playing around with something my father used to do. He was a baker back in Canada. Anyway, I got to fooling around with the dough and the filling. And I kind of liked it. So I brought a few in to the nurses, as a thank-you after Justin was born. They liked them too, so long johns went on the menu."

Take product quality: When I ask him whether there are any other independent donut shops in the area, shops that he respects, Alex tells me that when he bought into the business, there were eleven independents in the Fall River area. "Everybody either went out of business," Alex says, "or they went for the sandwich and coffee market. And now the big guys have ceded the quality to me."

This last observation comes off as a confession, as if Alex recognizes the burden and doesn't quite know whether he will bear up under the load. "My place has become a destination," he says, as car doors slam in the parking lot and three towheads scamper through the front door.

"Most of my customers travel for these donuts. Maybe they grew up here and moved away. Maybe they heard about our long johns and want to give them a try. You see their faces light up when they walk through the door. And you know it's got to be good. You know that you can't let them down."

Black Raspberry Long Johns

Inspired by Butler's—with an assist from James Beard's American Cookery*—this recipe requires your time and, above all else, your attention. Don't try and tell me that watching dough rise is the baker's equivalent of watching grass grow. I have already felt your pain, many times over. From my vantage, here on the other side, I can tell you that the result justifies the tedium. With the exception of a trek to West-port, Connecticut, I can't think of a better way to pass the morning hours than mixing and proofing, frying and stuffing these gossamer rectangles of dough.*

- 1 package (2¼ teaspoons) active dry yeast
- 2 tablespoons warm water
- ½ cup sugar, plus 1 teaspoon for the cream
- 1 cup whole milk
- 1 large egg, beaten
- 3½ cups all-purpose flour, sifted
- 2 tablespoons unsalted butter, melted
- 1 pint whipping cream for filling
- ½ gallon peanut or vegetable oil for frying
- Black raspberry jam, homemade or the best store-bought you can find

(continued)

In a small bowl, stir the yeast into the warm water. Add the ½ cup sugar and mix well. Set aside for 15 minutes for the yeast to dissolve. Meanwhile, scald the milk in a small saucepan. (Milk is scalded when it reaches about 180°F, or when you notice bubbles forming around the edge of the milk in the pan.) The milk should be luke-warm when you stir in the egg, the flour, and the yeast mixture together in a large mixing bowl. Bring the dough together, gathering it with your hands, until it is, as Beard would have it, "springy."

Brush the dough with the melted butter and cover with a sheet of wax paper. Set aside in a warm corner of the kitchen to rise for 1 to 1½ hours, until the dough doubles in bulk. On a lightly floured surface, roll out the dough with a rolling pin into a ½-inch-thick large rectangle. Then cut into rectangles that are 1 to 2 inches wide and 3 to 4 inches long. Set aside to rise again until almost doubled. Meanwhile, whip the cream until stiff, adding the remaining teaspoon of sugar at the end.

Pour the oil into a heavy cast-iron Dutch oven or other deep, heavy-bottomed pot until it reaches a depth of 3 inches. Heat the oil over medium-high heat to 375°F. Slip the long johns in and fry for 1 to 2 min-utes, flipping once, until golden. Remove with a slot-ted spoon and drain on wire racks. Once the long johns have cooled enough to be handled, slit them along the side and smear the cottony insides with jam. Spoon a generous portion of whipped cream atop the jam, press lightly to close, and serve. *Makes about 24 long johns*

Cuffs and Coffee

Paul Barry doesn't think much of Dunkin' Donuts. "They're shit," he tells me. "Nothing but warm shits, falling off a conveyor belt, one shit at a time. But hey, they were the wave. So I got out. Gave them my old location, negotiated ten percent of the gross receipts in rent. So go ahead, get yourself a large Coolatta. That's fine by me—I'll get my money and you'll get your shit."

Barry and I are in his office, a scruffy warren at the rear of Doughboy Police and Fire Supply, set in the Cranberry Crossing Shopping Center in the Boston suburb of Kingston. Two blackout SUVs block the fire lane out front. The showroom immediately adjacent is stocked with mirror-polished belts and camouflage-clad teddy bears. Not to mention Hero's Pride brand police whistles, yellow police tape, clip-on ties, and belt-clip baton holders. Everyone who walks through the door smells like well-oiled leather. And their shoes squeak.

As Barry, a large man with a burr haircut and a raspy voice, scarfs a Big Mac, he sketches the story of how he came to peddle first long johns, then handcuffs and nightsticks. "I opened up Doughboy in 1978," he tells me. "At one point I had nine locations. They were community centers, places where people came together. Working behind the counter was like working a bar full of sober people. My customers were my friends, they told good stories, and there were no drunk assholes.

"People got their own coffee," Barry recalls. "They would pour a round for the house when they got theirs. You would see the best of people in a donut shop, the kind of compassion for their neighbor that they usually manage to keep hidden. Plus, people don't go into a donut shop to sulk; they got bars for that."

Time, however, was not on Barry's side. "I figured out early on that this wasn't a long-term business," he says. "This was during the late '80s, during the recession, and companies were cracking down. They started telling their people to quit making runs to the corner donut shop. They told them, 'No coffee and donuts in the afternoon.' And then there was Dunkin' Donuts. They were buying up everybody, smothering the market.

"I remember when we started to make the move," he says, reaching deep in his bag for the last of his fries, dabbing his chin free of Special Sauce. "Our Dorchester location was the hub for everything. We were central to four or five different police precincts. We had the state police nearby, the transit police; they were all there. I thought, 'What's the easiest way to make more dollars?' By selling trinkets, that's how. So I started out selling patches. I set this lady up, sewing them on, right by the honey-dip machine. Pretty soon, this guy asks me, 'Paul, can you get me handcuffs, can you get me whistles?' Before I knew what I was doing, I was selling uniforms and we were storing boots in the walk-in."

Soon, Barry sold off the other locations and Doughboy Doughnuts begat Doughboy Police and Fire Supply. He kept the slogan Cuffs and Coffee. But he no longer served honey-dipped crullers. Barry hasn't looked back. Today, in addition to being the haberdasher of choice for law-enforcement officers throughout the city of Boston, Barry sells shoes to the U.S. Marshals Service and batons to police officers in Saudi Arabia. And he's built a steady business as a Hollywood costumer, outfitting the likes of John Travolta and Tommy Lee Jones for big-budget action flicks.

Sure, the name of his company still invites a few sniggers. But Barry is a big boy; he can take care of himself. A few years back, a gang of lawyers representing Pillsbury took exception to the name of his company and the roly-poly mascot on his sign. "Some firm with nineteen names on its letterhead called me from New York," Barry recalls. "They were nothing but weenie-whackers. They sent me nine registered letters before I would call them back. 'You're using our logo, they told me.' And I told them, 'You want to take me on? We'll be on the six-o'clock news together. Pillsbury and me. You're going to look like an asshole, explaining how I'm affecting your sale of Cheerios.'"

Eventually, Barry took the doughboy logo off his sign. (He retains the doughy icon on his business cards.) Barry harbors no grudges. Not with Pillsbury. Not even with Dunkin' Donuts. Turns out he doesn't so much dislike Dunkin' Donuts as he believes that the company lacks respect for their place, their product. "I went by Dunkin' this morning," he tells me. "Got a muffin."

Looking back, Barry believes his transition from coffee to cuffs was elemental. "If contractors had been coming in my donut shop, I would have sold them hammers," he says. "But I had cops, so I sold them handcuffs. Now, don't get me wrong. I won't sell uniforms to male strippers or those Village People kind of people. I don't mess with that piddleshit. I've got my standards."

beyond
lent

he Pennsylvania Dutch have long marked Fat Tuesday by eating *fastnachts*. My friend William Woys Weaver, in *Pennsylvania Dutch Country Cooking*, prescribes a dough of mashed potatoes, various flours, and flaxseed cut into square cakes, poked with holes, fried—and eaten by dunking into bowls of molasses.

Yet Lent isn't the only holiday in which donuts play a part. Among Americans of German descent, jelly donuts have long been thought to bring good luck to those who eat them on New Year's Eve. Nor is Christianity the only religion that has adopted the donut. Over the past few decades, Jews living in the Israeli homeland have embraced *sufganiyot*, another jelly-filled doughnut, as a ceremonial food of Hanukah. Their rationale is that, like latkes, *sufganiyot* rely upon a scald in hot oil and thus pay homage to the second century B.C. rededication of the Holy Temple, during which the oil in the temple lamp lasted eight nights instead of the expected one.

In Jerusalem, where the *sufganiyot* tradition began in the early 1950s, bakeries are already expanding beyond fruit fillings, adding *dulce de leche*–filled *sufganiyot* and, for adults only, vodka-spiked *sufganiyot*. Here in America, although bakeries like Pastryland in the Boston suburb of Brookline are leading the charge, *sufganiyot* have the barest toehold.

Part of the problem for *fastnacht*s and *sufganiyot* is pronunciation. White-bread Americans have a hard time wrapping their tongues around the names of these treats. Can you imagine a rhyme? *Sufganiyot / Won't you try it?*

Polish *paczki* (pronounced punch-key or poonch-key) on the other hand, have a fighting chance to be the next breakthrough pastry. They have verve. They have style. The Polish Muslims, a satirical rock octet from Hamtramck, Michigan, saw the potential when they cut a single, "Paczki Day," set to the tune of "Yesterday" by the Beatles: "Paczki Day / All the tourists come Hamtramck's way / And I add ten pounds to what I weigh / Oh I believe in Paczki Day."

Born of the dictate to extinguish stores of sugar and lard and eggs during the forty-day season of Christian penitence known as Lent, *paczki* have, over the past couple of decades, come to be the signal food of Hamtramck, a Polish enclave set smack-dab in the middle of Detroit. Hamtramck bakeries sell *paczki* all year long, but during Lent they roll out richer fillings and add extra sugar and egg yolks to the dough.

And as the Polish Muslims note, the tourists flock to eat their fill of these jelly donut analogues. Oaza Bakery, one of the largest, cranks out more than 100,000 *paczki* in the week or so leading up to Ash Wednesday. They are not alone. The New Martha Washington Bakery, founded in 1925, as well as a few other family owner-fryers dish raspberry- and prune-flushed *paczki* by the thousands.

Inevitably a trade group has arisen to ensure the promulgation of *paczki*. The National Paczki Promotion Board has set its sights on breaching the dam of ethnicity. They even set up a *paczki* hotline, reachable by calling 800-884-1500. According to the woman who answered the phone, they were inspired by the success of *malassadas* in Hawaii and beignets in New Orleans: "Those were once Lenten foods too. And now look at them. Just look at them."

SEVEN

Belle Cala!
Tout Chaud!

he pigeons are strung out on sugar, pecking the slate ter-
race like avian addicts, high on drifts of white powder:
black and gray torsos, claret talons, and, always, at the tips of
their beaks, clumps of white. They peck then fly, peck then
fly, arcing briefly through the wireback chairs, alongside the
marble-toped tables; they thrum with ungainly energy, ca-
reening among the tourists who claim the Café Du Monde in
New Orleans's French Quarter as their situational salon—
where the coffee comes laced with chicory and perhaps hot
milk, and the fresh-from-the-fryer donuts are known, by dint
of tradition and French colloquialism, as "beignets."

It's a familiar scene, sketched by many a travel writer, lived
by many a traveler. To sit among the pigeons, listening to a
busker honk out a Louis Armstrong tune, is a rite of passage.

Even if decades have passed since you first secured a table and shooed a pigeon, the scene still resonates. (Even, I might add, in the wake of Hurricane Katrina.) And the beignets, dished by cadres of bow-tied servers, taste just the way you re-call: like pillows of doughy vacancy drenched in showers of confectioners' sugar, like childhood exultations emerging from roiling oil.

You might declare the preceding passage to be over-wrought, even overwritten. And you might be right. But give me this: when I talk of eating beignets and sipping café au lait at the Café Du Monde, you know of which I speak. And it stirs something within you, some frisson of delight. I re-spond in the same way. When I take a seat at Café Du Monde, I claim the littoral of New Orleans as my own.

And yet I have discovered that the Café Du Monde is not the only *friteur* in town. Until the early 1970s there were two beignet walkups in the Quarter, with the oldest and most renowned being Morning Call Coffee Stand. Problem was, when Morning Call moved to a strip mall in suburban Metairie, everyone forgot about them. Everyone, that is, except the locals.

A year or so back I paid a visit in the company of a bona fide local. The setting—across from a JCPenney, alongside a store called ShoeNami—was far from picturesque. But the interior shone with the patina of yesteryear; the waiters poured coffee and hot milk deftly from battered gooseneck pitchers; and the three-to-an-order beignets begged me to reappraise the supremacy of Café Du Monde.

Morning Call's beignets were blond in color. They tasted vaguely sour (in the manner of a San Francisco loaf). They were slightly chewy and wholly ethereal. Served with a shaker of powdered sugar so that I could exact my own arterial damage, they compelled me to broaden my horizons, to ponder anew beignets and all manner of other fried New Orleans sweets.

I was liberated. In no time I was scarfing king cake donuts and sweet potato soufflé–gorged donuts, Bananas Foster beignets, and praline-goosed beignets. It was easy to make the leap from beignets to donuts, for they are, at their core, the same darn thing: fried dough. Other leaps seemed possible.

I was on the verge of sugar shock when I made the leap from the realm of beignets and donuts to the fried New Orleans dough of my dreams. They're called *calas*. Unlike beignets, which are, by most anyone's measure, enjoying a white-tablecloth-restaurant renaissance, these roundish fritters of rice and yeast, eggs and sugar and spices have all but disappeared from New Orleans commerce. I say *all* but disappeared, because two restaurant purveyors remain.

The first, the Coffee Pot, is easily dismissed. It's a restaurant in its dotage, skewed to appeal to tourists. Plus they unnecessarily gussy up their *calas,* studding them with pecan bits and setting them adrift in maple syrup. (Local cane syrup might pass muster, but maple syrup from Vermont has no business on the plate.)

The other *calas* contender is Elizabeth's. It's a spic-and-span neighborhood joint, a retrofitted shotgun, set in the Bywater—a funky but rapidly gentrifying neighborhood, downriver from the French Quarter. Heidi Trull, who until recently ran the place with her husband, Joe, was a student of *calas,* a keeper of the stories that locals tell.

Ask Heidi about how *calas* came to be a part of the New Orleans vernacular and she would tell you a story of African American entrepreneurship. Like many an interpreter of New Orleans food culture, she could quote chapter and verse from the 1901 vintage *Picayune Creole Cookbook,* which calls for a batter of cooked rice, flavored with nutmeg, fried in lard.

What's more, Heidi could paint a scene from that same cookbook: "The *cala* woman was a daily figure in the streets till within the last two or three years," observed the *Picayune* editors. "She went her rounds in quaint bandana tignon, guinea blue dress, and white apron, and carried on her head a covered bowl in which were the dainty and hot *calas.* Her cry, *'Belle cala! Tout chaud!'* would penetrate the morning air, and the olden Creole cooks would rush to the doors to get the first, fresh hot *calas . . .*"

Heidi knew her history. But she did not shy from a bit of editorializing. "I like to tell the tourists that these Creole women had to work the streets selling *calas,*" she would say as a smile teased her lips. "They had to sell *calas* to support their deadbeat husbands." Though Heidi's husband was no dead-beat, chances were good that if Heidi had taken to the streets peddling *calas* like the Creole women of old, he might have embraced the inherent nobility of a life of leisure. As it was, until Heidi sold Elizabeth's and headed back to her native South Carolina, he worked side by side with his bride, dishing honest food at decent prices.

In the *cala*, the powdered sugar–dusted fritter, born of what the *Picayune Creole Cookbook* calls "olden" New Orleans, Heidi and Joe found their totem. And they were not alone. Lolis Eric Elie, a friend and guardian of Creole folkways, has sounded the clarion in various publications. So has my mentor Jessica Harris, grande dame of African American foodways scholars. And Poppy Tooker, the Slow Food Convivium leader in New Orleans, has made it her mission to revive the *cala* by way of the cooking school. For now, however, Elizabeth's is the sole commercial purveyor of merit in New Orleans, a distinction that the restaurant continues to enjoy, even after the departure of Heidi and Joe.

Picayune Beignets

Beignets, cross-listed in the 1936 edition of the Picayune Creole Cook Book *as "fritters," occupy five pages of text: "The most important rule to be observed in making fritters, whether of fruit or plain, is to have the batter of the proper consistency. This is particularly important in making fruit fritters. 'La Pâte à Beignets,' as the Creoles call the batter, must be of sufficient consistency to envelop in one single immersion the fruit or other substance with which it is intended to make the fritters." The* Picayune *lists apple, apricot, banana, cherry, elderflower, fig, vanilla, lemon, peach, pineapple, almond, and sherry, strawberry, as well as Madeira and orange flower water–stoked versions. Here's a place to start.*

- 1⅔ cups all-purpose flour
- ½ cup barley flour
- ¼ cup sugar
- 2 teaspoons baking powder
- ¼ teaspoon baking soda
- ¼ teaspoon salt
- ⅔ cup buttermilk, at room temperature
- 1 large egg, at room temperature

- 1 tablespoon unsalted butter, melted and cooled slightly
- 1 teaspoon vanilla extract
- ½ gallon vegetable oil for frying
- Powdered sugar for sprinkling

In a large mixing bowl, combine the all-purpose and barley flours, the sugar, baking powder, baking soda, and salt. Mix well. In a separate bowl, whisk together the buttermilk and egg, then add the melted butter and vanilla, mixing well. Add the liquid ingredients to the dry ingredients and mix well.

Divide the resulting dough into two balls. On a floured surface, knead each ball 10 to 20 times and roll out with a rolling pin into a 9 x 9-inch square that is ⅛ inch thick. Next, cut the big square into 12 small squares.

Pour the oil into a cast-iron Dutch oven or other deep, heavy-bottomed pot until it reaches a depth of 3 to 4 inches. Heat the oil over medium-high heat to 370°F. Fry 3 or 4 beignets at a time, turning once shortly after dropping them in the oil, for about 2 minutes total or until lightly browned on both sides. Remove with a slotted spoon and drain on paper. Sprinkle with powdered sugar and serve hot. *Makes 24 beignets*

Calas

Take a bite. Feel the al dente resistance of rice beneath your teeth. Discern the trace of nutmeg. Divine, in that bite, in that cala, *the complement of past and present, the savor of New Orleans. This recipe is adapted from one by my friend and mentor Jessica Harris, author of, among other books,* The Welcome Table. *She points out that* calas *were, in the New Orleans of days past, the "exclusive culinary preserve of African American cooks." And she sketches linguistic complements in coastal Georgia and South Carolina where, in the Gullah dialect,* kala *means rice.*

Note: The dough will need to rest overnight.

- ¾ cup uncooked long-grain rice
- 2¼ cups cold water
- 1½ packages (3⅜ teaspoons) active dry yeast
- ½ cup warm water
- 4 large eggs, beaten
- ⅓ cup granulated sugar
- ¾ teaspoon freshly grated nutmeg
- ¾ teaspoon salt
- 2 cups all-purpose flour

■ Canola oil for frying
■ Confectioners' sugar for dusting

In a medium saucepan, combine the rice and cold water and bring to a boil over high heat. Lower the heat to medium and cook for about 25 minutes or until the rice is soft. Drain the rice and dump into a large mixing bowl. With the back of a spoon, mash the rice to a pulp, then set aside to cool.

In a small bowl, dissolve the yeast in the warm water. Add the yeast mixture to the rice and beat with a fork for 2 minutes. Cover the bowl with a damp kitchen towel and set aside in a warm place to rise overnight.

Add the eggs, granulated sugar, nutmeg, salt, and flour to the rice mixture. Beat thoroughly with a fork, cover with a kitchen towel, and set aside for 30 minutes. Pour the oil into a cast-iron Dutch oven or other deep, heavy-bottomed pot until it reaches a depth of 3 inches. Heat the oil over medium-high heat to 375°F. Drop heaping tablespoons of dough into the oil and fry until nicely browned on both sides, about 1 to 2 minutes. Remove with a slotted spoon and drain on wire racks. Dust with confectioners' sugar and serve while still hot. *Makes about 24* **calas**

Gumbo Donuts

I've never been keen on the king cakes of New Orleans. Don't get me wrong. I like the tradition of gathering with friends during the days between the Feast of Epiphany and Mardi Gras to cut into a ring of brioche striped with green, yellow, and purple carnival sugars. And I'm as curious as the next fellow about who will bite into their slice and discover the plastic doll that custom dictates be secreted within. I appreciate that such a discovery not only deems the finder king for the duration of the week but also requires them to buy a king cake for next year's celebration.

My problem has always been that most king cakes have the moisture of porcelain, the savor of basalt. Sure, the late 1980s witnessed a king cake renaissance during which bakers started piping in various fillings, including praline-laced cream cheese. And yes, I have tried a so-called Zulu cake, made with chocolate dough, chocolate filling, and chocolate icing. But I never understood the true gastronomic appeal of the king cake until, acting on the advice of my friend Sara Roahen, I sought out Fay's Take-Out and Honey Whip Donuts in the New Orleans suburb of Gretna. In addition to year-round favorites like sweet potato purée–gorged donuts known euphemistically as "donut pies," owner Fay Antoine serves a king cake donut, a cinnamon-strafed hole-less orb with a strawberry jelly–filled depression at its center. Though she forgoes the secreting of a plastic baby within, she does dish a mean bowl of gumbo. Somehow that makes up for the omission.

EIGHT

Doppelgänger Donuts

hawaii is a culinary funhouse, a Creolized archipelago populated by Okinawan and Japanese, Polynesian and Portuguese, Korean and Chinese. This is the land of Spam *musubi*. Of Thanksgiving turkeys stuffed with Japanese *mochi* and Chinese sausage. Of burgers capped with kimchee.

On a weeklong ramble about Oahu and the Big Island, I ate my share—and more—of fiery kimchee burgers. By day two I was snacking on nori-bound tiles of rice and Spam retrieved from the hotbox of a corner convenience store. And though I arrived at the wrong time of the year to taste the local take on turkey, that didn't stop me from questioning a half-dozen local butchers about the possibility of an off-season special.

Secure in the knowledge that I would not find such comestibles on the mainland, I ate them with a fervor that borders upon desperation. But as the days slid by and my attitude and appetite matured, I began to realize that I made a serious miscalculation: I underestimated the import of *malassadas*.

Over the course of just four days, I had come to consider a breakfast of these sugar-and-cinnamon-dusted Portuguese donuts to be humdrum. I was lulled into a belief that while a taste for Spam *musubi* might be lost in translation from Hawaii to home, *malassadas* were not just translatable; they were interchangeable with mainland donuts. As to how I came to such an indefensible conclusion, I'm still not quite sure.

m y week began with great promise. I claimed an open mind, an empty stomach. At Leonard's, a 1952-vintage bakery on the island of Oahu, in the shadow of Waikiki, I ate my first *malassada*. I was primed. Although reared on the cottony goodness of Krispy Kreme, I had grown weary of the praise heaped on the brand. Call me sugar-fatigued. Call me pretentious. I don't care. Just know that I was craving something new, a donut of a different texture, a donut that was not born on an assembly line and glazed by way of a pneumatic waterfall.

The *malassada* at Leonard's was dense, even a tad undercooked. This made good sense when I learned that the word *malassada* translates from the Portuguese as something like "poorly cooked." At its core, this hole-less fritter was moist, almost creamy. It tasted as if the cook had yanked it from the oil when the eggy dough was still a nanosecond shy of its potential. It seemed that the cook knew—with the kind of sixth sense bequeathed only to true artisans—that if she allowed the donut to reach its apogee, mere mortals such as I could not endure the pleasure. Leonard's proved an appropriate place to begin my explorations, for most locals agree that founder Leonard Rego is the man who transformed the *malassada* from a homemade Lenten food of Portuguese derivation to a commercial bakery product embraced by Hawaiians of all ethnicities.

Nothing is simple, however, when it comes to matters of donut provenance. It seems that there is even debate about how *malassadas* came to be associated with Portugal. Some sources look to the Azores, a chain of islands in the Atlantic Ocean colonized by the Portuguese in hopes of raising cane for sugar. They argue that, far from home, cooks on the island of São Miguel began frying sweet bread dough originally intended for the bake oven. And they may be right. If so, the next step came in the mid-1800s, when Hawaiian plantation owners recruited laborers from Portuguese-controlled islands to work the sugar cane crops.

ut not all stories of *malassadas* are stories of Portugal. That same night, I ate dinner at Chef Mavro, a luxe Honolulu restaurant with the conservative curb appeal of an insurance brokerage. George Mavrothalassitis, a Frenchman, was at the helm. White damask napped my table. Zucchini blossoms emerged from the kitchen dusted with green tea. Foie gras arrived wrapped in a torchon of nori. And then my ten-buck *malassada* dessert appeared—a threesome of brioche balls, gorged with purple-fleshed passion fruit, dabbed with a guava coulis, and set adrift in a bowl of pineapple-coconut ice cream.

It was a high-wire act, a slummer's stunt executed with aplomb by a cocksure chef. And I loved every sticky morsel. But on a purely empirical level, Mavro's fritters were no match for the ones I tasted the next morning at nearby Champion Malassadas. Proprietor Joc Miw, a bright-eyed native of Macao who immigrated to Hawaii by way of Nicaragua, spoiled me. As I inhaled his 55-cent orbs of deep-fried bliss, a peculiar kind of Hawaiian ennui began to take hold.

Standing at his counter, my worldview skewed fatalistic. My horizon dimmed. Would I ever again taste as platonic a treat as this? Rather than resolve such a question, I affected an attitude of jaded indifference that blossomed into my aforementioned *malassada* miscalculation.

While I waited for the funk to pass, I ate all manner of Hawaiian foods. Poi and poke. *Lomi lomi* and *jook*. Soursops and rambutans. Moon cakes and waffle dogs.

Nothing broke the spell. Not a trip to Agnes Portuguese Bake Shop on the windward side of Oahu, in downtown Kailua, where, with baker Non DeMello by my side, I tasted the most texturally compelling *malassadas* of the trip. Not even an expedition to Tex's Drive-In on the Big Island, home of the single best reason to book a flight to Hawaii—a creamy *malassada* jiggered with, among other chutney-like fillings, pineapple, papaya, guava-strawberry or—that paragon of sweetness, that archetype of heat—pepper jelly.

And then, on my last day in town, I returned to Leonard's. As I sat on a bench out front, sipping a cup of coffee and nibbling my second *malassada* of the morning, a rail-thin man in a starburst print Hawaiian shirt came loping through the parking lot, a box of donuts tucked under his arm. I wasn't expecting my doppelgänger.

He snagged a seat alongside me and pointed back down Kapahulu Avenue where, less than a block away, one of those hybridized stores stands. Left-hand side: Dunkin' Donuts. Right-hand side: Baskin-Robbins. "Got to establish a baseline experience," he said, sliding a Dunkin' Donuts box my way.

I reached for one. I took a bite. And then another. Sugar and caffeine found their mark. My head cleared. My focus returned. And I tossed what was left of his donut toward the trash can. When it caromed off the rim and landed in the parking lot, I fished a dollar bill from the pocket of my shorts and followed my friend inside.

While waiting for a hot batch to emerge from Leonard's fryer, I told the man of the halogen smile of Joc Miw; I told him of Non DeMello's deft touch. I regaled him with tales of mornings spent scarfing pepper jelly–girded *malassadas* on the Big Island, and afternoon detours to Kailua, and nights of purple passion fruit indulgence in Honolulu. And as I bit into what passes for a donut hereabouts, I warned him of the evils of jaded indifference.

Malassadas

This recipe comes from Agnes Portuguese Bake Shop, the most traditional malassada *vendor in Hawaii. Non DeMello, co-proprietor and chief fry cook, is a font of* malassada *lore and one of the few Hawaiians I met who had traveled to Portugal and tasted* malassadas *in situ. While many people I met were fixed on a* malassada *definition that precluded the presence of a hole, Non is not so rigid. I've come to think of the divots in the centers of his* malassadas *as vestigial holes. Or is it the other way around?*

- 1 package (2¼ teaspoons) active dry yeast
- 1 teaspoon granulated sugar
- ¼ cup warm water
- 8 cups all-purpose flour
- ½ teaspoon salt
- 6 large eggs, beaten
- ¼ cup mashed potatoes
- 1 cup evaporated milk (from one 8-ounce can)
- 4 tablespoons unsalted butter, melted and slightly cooled

■ 1 cup cold water
■ ½ gallon vegetable oil for frying, plus a little extra
■ Powdered sugar for topping

In a small bowl, dissolve the yeast and sugar in the ¼ cup warm water, stir to combine, and set aside for 5 minutes for the mixture to foam.

In a large mixing bowl, sift the flour and salt together. All at once, add the eggs, mashed potatoes, evaporated milk, melted butter, and 1 cup cold water, stirring to combine. Add the yeast mixture and incorporate thoroughly, stirring until the dough becomes tacky.

Cover the dough with a kitchen towel and set aside to rise in a warm place until doubled, about 1½ hours. Punch down and allow to rise again. Pour the oil (reserving a bowl of cold oil for wetting your fingers) into a cast-iron Dutch oven or other deep, heavy-bottomed pot until it reaches a depth of 3 to 4 inches. Heat the oil over medium-high heat to 375°F. Dip your fingertips in the bowl of oil and pinch off golf ball–sized lumps of dough, using your thumb to make a divot in the center of each. You can also use a small ice cream scoop dipped in oil to extract the dough. Fry, turning once, for 2 to 3 minutes or until browned

(continued)

on both sides. Remove from the oil with a slotted
spoon, roll in powdered sugar, and set on wire racks
to drain. *Makes about 50* malassadas

Note: If you desire filled malassadas *of the sort Big Tex serves, forgo
the thumbprint at the center of your dough balls. After frying, fill a
turkey baster with your favorite pepper jelly, and well, you can take
it from there.*

Cambodian Donut Dreams

for Angelenos on the make, donuts offer entrée to the opposite sex. To be more specific, in my limited experience donut statistics are standards of cross-gender cocktail banter. One night, at a party in the Hollywood Hills, I overheard a guy with tousled hair tell a girl with bangled earrings that Los Angeles has more donut shops than any other city in the nation. That translates to one for every seven thousand citizens, he said. She batted her eyes, not once, but twice. He took that as a sign.

A more reliable way for the donut-obsessed playboy to angle into conversation might be to inquire as to sweet young thing's take on Buddhism. For everyone knows that Buddhism—along with Scientology—is the lingua franca of post-millennial L.A. But few sweet young things with a yen for enlightenment know that Buddhists, more specifically Cambodian refugees, a goodly number of whom practice Buddhism, may own as many as 80 percent of the independent donut shops in Los Angeles. Such knowledge, and a little Leonard Cohen on the stereo, will get you far. That's what I would tell tousle boy, if he asked.

———————

by most accounts, the Cambodian donut dream took hold in Los Angeles in the mid-1970s, at about the same time that Pol Pot became prime minister of Cambodia. His reign was bloody. Executed, starved, or overworked, more than two million of the seven million people in Cambodia were dead by 1980. Of the lucky few who managed to escape, more than 200,000 fled for the United States. Forty-five thousand or so of those settled in Los Angeles. By some estimates, more than two thousand of those would enter the donut business.

The rapidity of their flight and the recentness of their arrival are exceptional. But the story of an American immigrant group's adoption of a single industry is of long note. Think of Greek pizza parlors. Or Vietnamese nail salons.

The donut industry offered low start-up costs. (At the time many Cambodian refuges alighted on these shores, you could be in business for $20,000 to $40,000.) What's more, donuts are, by and large, a cash business, free of billing and receivables headaches. Then there was the matter of family. Like the Greeks, Cambodians realized that a family-run restaurant benefits from exceptionally low labor costs. And when it comes time to eat, the whole family eats at wholesale prices.

An informal series of business transactions cemented the Cambodian hold on the industry. An uncle with three donut shops would advance a nephew the money to buy his first. And soon enough that nephew would have five, one of which he would be willing to sell to his second cousin at below market rates. That's the shorthand version of how Ning Yen came to be a donut mogul.

Born on a farm, Yen lived with his parents and seven siblings until the Khmer Rouge seized their acreage in 1975. For the next four years, Yen worked the rice fields at the behest of the Khmer Rouge, oftentimes living on a scavenger's diet. In 1979, he fled Cambodia, making his way to the United States. A few months later he won a job at a Winchell's Donuts in Santa Ana. By 1984, Yen bought his own place, Mag's Donuts, in Irvine. Within a few years, he owned a chain of seven donut shops. Today he is a principal in B&H Distributors, a wholesaler of dough mix, sugar, and icings to independent donut shops.

If you had stopped in for a donut during those early years, it's unlikely you would have discerned anything remotely *Cambodian* about Yen's operation. French crullers; peanut-crowned chocolate cake; chocolate-raised, showered with coconut; cinnamon-raised, twisted like a cheroot: Mag's sold the standards.

But if you had a chance to peek around back, in the living quarters or maybe the anteroom alongside the office, you would have likely spied a Buddhist shrine with a cross-legged holy one at the center. And chances are that if you stop in an independent donut shop in Los Angeles today, you will find shrines there too.

Perhaps the shop owners, many of whom rise at one or two in the morning to work eighteen-hour days, recognize their plights in the Buddhist belief that suffering is inseparable from existence. Maybe they believe that the extinction of worldly desires, as advocated by the Buddha's teachings, comes easiest for a man who falls dead asleep before the sun sets.

i had planned on sharing these insights with tousle boy. But it seems he doesn't require that kind of enlightenment. On my way out the door, I catch sight of him and bangle girl. They are cooing on the couch. I stop to say my good-byes. Her sandals are off and he is massaging her instep. Spread on her lap is a copy of *Los Angeles* magazine, open to a full-page, four-color photographic shooting gallery of thirty donuts commonly found in Los Angeles.

Catalogued as they are, like butterflies pinned to whiteboard, the donuts evince a certain luridness, a psychosexual sheen that owes as much to the various shapes as it does to the cherry glaze on a nutmeg cake or the puddle of vanilla pudding at the core of a Bavarian chocolate crème. As I cross the threshold, I look back over my shoulder. Tousle boy is gesturing in the general direction of a chocolate twist bar.

california
dalliance

Stan Berman, proprietor of Stan's Donuts in Westwood Village, a hacienda-style shopping district adjacent to Beverly Hills, is in the mood to talk. Stan is in his sixties. His hair is white, his humor good. It's ten in the morning. The last customer exited with a plain cake and a bubble tea. I'm eating a jelly-style yeast-raised donut, nibbling my way toward the Reese's Cup at the center.

"I fried my first donut at age six," he tells me, leaning against the glass display case stocked with devil's food cakes, raisin-buttermilk bars, and yeast donuts stuffed with fresh bananas and peanut butter and glazed with a rocky road of chocolate chips. "I was working for my father, Frank A. Berman and Sons. He worked an open kettle, didn't do that many donuts. Maybe six or seven dozen a day. There was no thermostat on that thing; you checked the oil by sprinkling in water and listening for the crackle and spritz."

In the 1950s, Berman moved west. Philadelphia was stodgy, old world. California was a place of soaring blue skies and infinite possibilities. To Stan's way of thinking, donuts were emblematic of California. Cheap and quick and modern, like the suburbs that sprawled through the hills, donuts were a dalliance. He told himself, *A man does not make a life out of donuts.*

Berman bought his corner shop in 1965. "We started out using help from a sorority house at UCLA," he says. "They worked out the schedule. We'd get one hour from one girl, three hours from another. We sold donuts from a pass-thru window. Pretty old-fashioned stuff. Mom-and-pop kind of stuff."

As Los Angeles grew, so did Stan's. A few years later, he bought out the Orange Julius stand next door. Before long, Hollywood came calling. When the film *Love Story* debuted, says Stan, "Ali MacGraw and Steve McQueen would sit out front on his motorcycle, watching the crowds file into the Westwood Fox across the street.

"We've had everybody in here," he continues. "This woman who worked for Imelda Marcos used to come in and buy three or four dozen at a time. I've had porn kings with half-dozen-a-day habits. You ever heard of Al Goldstein, the guy who published *Screw* magazine? He ate so many we started calling the peanut butter donut the 'Al.'"

Celebrities aside, Berman tells me that the donut business in California is no different from anywhere else. He admits that the people of Los Angeles are a peculiar lot, but he doesn't ascribe to the Hollyweird stories. "That's too easy," he says. "My business is still mom and pop. There's no need to make this into something it isn't."

To emphasize his point, Stan hefts a bag of BakeMark donut mix onto a work table. "All we do is add water and yeast," he says. "To get our quality, we're careful about how we handle the dough. And we work in small batches. The secret is that no more than an hour should pass between the mixer and the fryer. If you wait too long, the dough turns flat. And when you drop them in the oil, your donuts don't bounce like they should."

I arrived intent upon drawing sweeping conclusions. I figured there was some truth to be gleaned from the conjunction of crullers and California. But Berman isn't having it. Sure, he knows that few donut shops claim porn kings as regular customers. "I'll give you that much," he says. But he makes a convincing argument against the Californication theory of the donut. "I'm running a neighborhood donut shop," says Berman, as he steps to the cash register, his hand outstretched to greet an old friend. "Isn't that enough?"

NINE

Humbled by a Berry

the strawberries flash in the morning sun like rubies, their color deep, their contours faceted. I lean toward the case, pressing my nose against the plate glass. The crowd behind me churns with impatience. I hear grumbles, muffled curses, promises of assistance.

I stand my ground and scan the shelf once more, my eyes tracking back and forth like a first-generation copy machine. *Bottom right,* I tell myself, stooping to meet the gaze of the woman on the other side of the transom, *bottom right.* But when she asks for my order, I return to scan mode, pinging across the tray of strawberry donuts, my mind paralyzed by the possibilities, unable to translate want into action. So she just hands me one, a random grab, luck of the paw.

I retreat to one of the two benches set in the shade of

a faux-mansard roof and, with my back to the stutter and whoosh of the morning commute, I begin to deconstruct my prize. But first I hold the donut high, appraising the lurid cluster of berries bulging from a yeast-raised pout of dough.

Jim Nakano stands at the back of his Donut Man shop, a block-and-glass rectangle on Route 66—yes, that Route 66—in the suburb of Glendora, east of Los Angeles. The San Gabriel Mountains loom in the distance, past the strip malls. He wears a white polo shirt and white pants. A white apron carries just short of his knees. Reading glasses dangle from a chain around his neck. His hair is black, his smile easy.

I'm merely one of the seekers, the folks who arrive each spring in search of strawberry donuts, each summer in search of peach. Granted, not every seeker shows up with a reporter's notebook in his back left pocket, a digital camera in his front right, and eats his donut while perusing a color-coded spreadsheet listing the top twenty donut shops in greater Los Angeles. But Nakano knows what to expect. My queries will be no different from any soul who happens upon the perfect strawberry donut and wonders how it came to be.

Nakano knows what I want to hear. And, with not much more than a nod from me, he slides on the bench to tell his story. Born in 1940, he grew up in East L.A., the son of second-generation Japanese-Americans who spent the World War II years in an internment camp. Like so many of the nation's best donut shop operators, he did not anticipate this life. After college, he set out to be a company man, climbing the rungs at JCPenney. But by the time he was thirty, Nakano realized his ascent was not to be swift, so he bailed. Nakano wanted to be his own boss, to plot his own trajectory. And the cheapest business he could get into was donuts.

Among the generation of owners who came into the donut business during the franchise boom of the 1960s and '70s, Nakano's low-cost refrain is a constant. Nakano knew the drill: a mixer, a proofer, a fryer, an address, and you're in business. Draft your family as employees. Stretch your sugar glazes with water. Buy your first bag of mix from the franchisor with your savings, your second bag with the profits from the previous day. And pray that the customers come.

Yet Nakano never adopted the customary tack. He decided to follow the lead of bakers, not fellow donut men. "I figured that if I knew how to make bread, I could make donuts," he says. "But I knew that might not be enough." As I finish my donut and reach for two of the berries that slipped from their berth, he sketches the moment in 1974 when he found his métier.

"I knew there was something else, a way to distinguish myself," says Nakano. "I discovered the strawberry donut in conversation with a friend. He runs Commacho Farms, down valley from here. At that point we were doing strawberry donuts like anyone else, piping in a filling I bought from my supplier."

He continues, "My friend and I, we were talking about something, maybe about how early we both had to get up. He was telling me about picking strawberries while they were plump, before the sun gets to them. I was telling him about getting up in the middle of the night to fry donuts. And it hit me—strawberry donuts, real strawberry donuts."

b y this time, our conversation has moved from the bench to Nakano's kitchen. Were it not for the crates of fruit stacked on a nearby counter, it would look like a hundred other donut kitchens in greater Los Angeles. "I start with a donut," he says, working a stubby knife into the side of a fist-sized and hole-less pouf of fried dough. "Instead of injecting it with filling, I take five or six strawberries, dip them in glaze and lay them in the pocket."

Nakano is proud of his doughs. He uses five different mixes, depending upon the donut. French for crullers. Devil's food for the twisted cheroots he calls "tiger tails." Buttermilk bars get a sweeter, old-fashioned dough. And so on. "I take pains to do it right," he says, handing the finished strawberry donut my way. "I make good doughs and I fry in soybean oil. But I know that donuts are one thing. Even good ones like mine. They're one thing. But beautiful fruit," he says, cradling a fat strawberry in his hand, "beautiful fruit like this deserves something more."

Nakano reaches for three more strawberries. He bids me to come close. "You see the leaves on these berries? See them? They have not even begun to wilt. This morning, they were still in the ground. They're perfect. They're humbling. That's a heck of a thing for a man to say, isn't it? Humbled by a little red berry. But there you have it."

In the world according to Jim Nakano, the donut is conveyance for a natural phenomenon. And that may well be enough. Let everyone else boast of secret formulas and proprietary mixes, says Nakano. He knows that the great majority of California donut shops get their mix from one or two makers. He knows the work he puts into his product. But he's not one to boast. "I know satisfaction," he says.

Nakano knows the joy of watching customers walk away cradling a clamshell of fresh fried dough in their hands, peering into a brace of strawberries that spill forth as if from a cornucopia. That's the way they all leave him, their eyes fixed upon the berries as they walk away. And that's the way I leave him, staring down at my prize.

Farmers' Market Purse Donuts

Make these before you go to bed on a Friday night in the spring of the year. On Saturday morning, make a mad dash for your local farmers' market. If strawberries are coming in, buy at least a couple quarts. Same thing with blueberries, blackberries, whateverberries. If it's later in the year and you live in the land of peaches, well, buy some peaches. Nectarines might work nice, too. Mangoes, if you can find them fresh. Point is to make a filling of whatever berry or fruit is at its peak.

Note: The dough will need to rest overnight.

DONUTS

- 1 package (2¼ teaspoons) active dry yeast
- ½ cup warm water
- 3½ cups all-purpose flour
- ¾ cup sugar
- Scant teaspoon salt
- 2 large eggs, separated (reserve the whites in the refrigerator for assembly)
- 3 tablespoons unsalted butter, softened
- ½ gallon peanut or vegetable oil for frying

FILLING

- 2 tablespoons sugar
- 1 cup water
- Juice of 1 lemon
- 2 quarts hulled strawberries or other fresh berries

In a small bowl, dissolve the yeast in the warm water, stir to combine, and set aside for 5 minutes for the mixture to foam.

In a large mixing bowl, combine the flour, sugar, salt, and egg yolks, mixing well. Pour the yeast mixture into the flour mixture and mix until a dough forms.

Lightly flour a work surface and dump the dough out. Knead in 2 tablespoons of the butter and continue kneading until the dough is no longer sticky. With the remaining tablespoon of butter, grease another large bowl, dump the dough in, and turn the dough to coat in the butter. Cover with plastic wrap and place in the refrigerator overnight.

In the morning, pull the dough out of the refrigerator, remove the wrap, and let it come to room temperature. That should take 30 minutes or so.

Meanwhile, make the filling: In a small saucepan, make a simple syrup by combining the sugar with the water in a small saucepan over medium heat and heating to a simmer. Stir until the sugar is incorporated and the mixture is somewhat viscous. Add the lemon juice and set aside to cool. *(continued)*

Flour a work surface and roll out the dough with a rolling pin to a thickness of about ⅛ inch. Using a wide-mouth glass or a 2- or 3-inch pastry cutter, punch out 20 or so rounds. Gather the scraps and reroll as necessary, cutting out about another 12 rounds, working to get an even number.

Lightly grease two baking sheets with butter or shortening. In a small bowl, beat the two egg whites. Arrange rows of dough rounds on the trays. Brush the edges of the rounds with egg white and top with a second round. Press the two halves to seal along the periphery—do not mash them together. Repeat again and again, setting the completed donuts aside to rise for about 20 minutes.

Pour the oil into a cast-iron Dutch oven or other deep, heavy-bottomed pot until it reaches a depth of 3 to 4 inches. Heat the oil over medium-high heat to 360°F. Working in batches of 3 or 4, slide the donuts into the oil. Cook, turning once, for about 2 minutes, or until golden on both sides. Remove with a slotted spoon, drain on wire racks, and cool for 10 to 15 minutes. With a sharp knife, slit the donuts open, working to free a pocket at the core. Ladle in berries and syrup, stuffing until the donuts are just shy of overflowing.

Makes 18 to 20 donuts

A Nest of Midgets

there are many ways to parse the donut spectrum. Cake or yeast seems the most obvious. But there are others. Take packing. Me, I'm particular about how a clerk packs donuts for travel. I don't like bags.

In California, I meet many a compatriot who believes as I do that fragile pastries won't endure rough handling. Stuffed harum-scarum in a bag, one atop the other, chocolate glazed in full frontal contact with a trio of raspy cinnamon-dusted lovelies or a lone jimmy-sprinkled, great donuts run the risk of losing their sugar-slicked patina.

Keeping such matters top of mind, I like to eat my donuts on my feet or at the counter. Handed over one at a time, preferably tucked in a Midget brand tissue (one of those diaphanous white sleeves stocked by better shops), a great donut has a chance of maintaining its fresh-from-the-glazer sheen.

For those times I must travel with donuts, I look for a shop that packs flat. I've learned the hard way that a lateral filing system is fine for a box of books but, like the infernal bag, just shy of ruinous for donuts. Need I even tell you that Jim Nakano swaddles his strawberry donuts in a nest of Midgets and lays them out like estate jewelry?

Now if I could just get him to stock those soft pink boxes I came to know while eating at lesser donut stands in southern California. Hold them up in the right light, canted open to reveal a regiment of pastel-frosted rounds, and they recall a Wayne Thiebaud painting.

TEN

Hey! Donut Man!

mark Carter, onetime proprietor of Carter's Doughnuts, "where every day is Fry-day," is a product of
the clean-living California gestalt. "I was eating whole-grain
everything by the time I was three," he told me, back in the
spring of 2004. "My mother denied me any food that was
fried. She believed all American pop food was baseless, that it
was bad for you. And to a certain degree I bought into that,"
said Carter, a forty-something-year-old with a rail-thin body
and an angular face. "I didn't adopt her dictates wholesale
but they affected what I ate, who I was."

As Mark told it, his mother's dismissal of Americana begat
a kind of snobbery. "I always said donuts were trash," Carter
said. "Then I'm at this pastry chef event in Los Angeles. And
this woman promises to bring donuts. 'Really good donuts,'

she says. And she's right, they were amazing. They were from Bob's, the stand in the L.A. Farmers Market. That's when my eyes opened, when the donut line of demarcation became clear to me. Shame on me for dismissing donuts out of hand. On one side there's trash, but on the other there's Bob's."

Carter and I sat at a table on the sidewalk outside Flying Goat Coffee Shop, ninety miles north of San Francisco in Santa Rosa, California. Between us was a flip-top pastry box filled with Carter's creations. I'd already eaten a pancake donut with maple frosting and begun nibbling at a filled donut, plush with syrah grape, and a yeast-raised donut, lacquered with Dagoba organic chocolate.

By this point in our conversation, I knew that Carter used fresh eggs and butter in his pastries. I knew that he used organic and unrefined flours and sugars. I knew that he acquired his chocolate from fair-trade sources and cooked his donuts in nonhydrogenated shortening that is blissfully free of trans fats, which, as every heart-healthy American knows, are associated with a higher risk of heart disease.

I had grown weary of what sounded to me like a let's-save-the-donut-from-itself campaign. I sought Carter out because I believed him to be a man obsessed by donuts. I didn't come looking for a lecture. And then, right about the time I was deciding Carter is a prig, he leveled with me.

"I know I can't make a convincing argument that donuts are good for you," he said. "And I'm not going to try. You can't get away from fat. Donuts are fried in fat. We're not dogs; fat doesn't make our coats shinier. But fat—good fat, good shortening like I use—makes for a good donut. This is about wonderful pastry. You don't eat my donuts because of what's in them. I'm not going to try and convert the people who love Winchell's to my donuts. I just want to make a great donut. I make donuts for the people of northern California. And that means I crack eggs instead of opening a bag of mix. I melt butter. That's what they want. You can call my donuts organic, but that's too easy. That's not what I'm after."

The market would be different downstate. Donuts in Los Angeles are a commodity, said Carter. And he was probably right. Although I would cite the Donut Man of Glendale as the exception rather than Bob's, whose cake donuts I find to be austere and whose dinosaur- and kitty-shaped donuts I suspect to be born of a mix.

In the days before donuts became his focus, Carter worked as a pastry chef at some of Los Angeles's best restaurants. And for a while in the 1990s he was chef-owner of Duplex, which he describes as an "urban roadhouse." He won praise for his pastry work and, on occasion, fried donuts from brioche dough scraps. But he did not come to see the true possibilities until he moved to Santa Rosa in 1994.

"Like everybody else, I wanted out of L.A.," he recalled. "And I wanted something that was my own. I sold wine for a while. I pulled the corks and listened to people say, 'Another great vintage,' but all I could tell them was, 'I'll pass along your compliments to the winemaker.'"

Then he noticed Krispy Kreme. And he remembered his love of Bob's. He saw his chance. "You watch them make your donut at Krispy Kreme," said Carter. "You watch it roll out all glazed and beautiful, and in that time spent watching, it becomes *your* donut. Now if you have to wait twenty minutes for that donut, it's only natural that you seek parity between your time invested and the payoff so you buy a dozen when all you want is two. I mean who's going to face down the counterman at a Krispy Kreme after waiting in line and order two hot donuts? Order two and you look like a jackass. That's a business for me."

From early 2002 through late 2003, Carter worked to perfect his dough. He opened the week of Christmas in 2003, starting with a handful of wholesale accounts and no retail business. "I don't know where the business is going," said Carter. "The business itself will tell me what to do; I'm merely the shepherd—and the fry cook."

Flying Goat, where we sat and talked, was a typical outlet buying a few dozen a day at each of its three Sonoma County locations. When Carter came in the door, the barista yelled, "Hey! Donut man!" From the wings a young boy approached, donut in hand, and asked, "Did you really *make* this?"—as if the concept of an artisanal donut was beyond his ken. And Carter smiled wide. "In Los Angeles, my donuts would be a novelty," he told me later. "I would be a freak. Here I hope people will see them for what they are, as—oh, I don't know— progressive donuts, great donuts, donuts from northern California."

In his syrah jelly donut, Carter came closest to achieving the northern California ideal: a pastry that evokes what the French (and a goodly number of local winemakers) call *ter-*

roir, a pastry that the donut-loving Pennsylvania Dutch call *bodegeschmack,* a pastry that offers a taste of the land and the goods that come from the land. For what could taste more of the land, in a region where grapes are the foremost agricultural crop, than a donut piped with jelly made from local grapes?

I asked Carter, point blank, why he fell for donuts. He'd been hinting at it all along. But his answers had been oblique. I had expected Carter to quote Marie-Antoine Carême, the founder of modern French cuisine. I could almost hear the words forming in the back of his mind. "Most noble of all the arts is architecture," said Carême, "and its greatest manifestation is the art of the pastry chef."

But Carter surprised me. His passions were more direct, his pleasures more sensual. "I've always loved science," he said. "And I've always loved visuals. So I love watching foods as they change from one state to another. Donuts start out as a highly viscous substance that, when it hits oil, turns into a cake. That fascinates me, that captivates."

Pancake Donut with Frosted Maple Syrup

Unfortunately, the oil-induced transformation of dough did not prove captivating to Carter's fellow citizens. A boom in the sale of "better" donuts never materialized. In the summer of 2005, Carter ceased operations, leaving the folks at Flying Goat pining for a bit of bodegeschmack. *Consider the following Carter-inspired glaze to be a taste of what might have been.*

- ½ cup (1 stick) unsalted butter, softened
- ¾ cup sugar
- 1 teaspoon vanilla extract
- 3 large eggs, at room temperature
- 4 cups self-rising flour
- ½ teaspoon ground cinnamon
- ¼ teaspoon salt
- 1 cup buttermilk
- ½ gallon peanut or vegetable oil for frying

FROSTING

- 8 tablespoons (1 stick) unsalted butter, softened
- ½ cup maple syrup
- 3 cups confectioners' sugar

(continued)

In a large bowl, cream the butter and sugar with an electric mixer. When the mixture loses its grittiness, add the vanilla. Stir in the eggs one at a time. In another large bowl, combine the flour, cinnamon, and salt. Dump the dry ingredients into the creamed egg and butter. Add the buttermilk, a little at a time, and mix until the dough begins to get tacky. Cover with a kitchen towel and set aside to rest for 30 minutes.

Meanwhile, make the frosting: In a medium bowl, cream the butter and maple syrup together. Gradually add the confectioners' sugar, mixing after each addition to thoroughly incorporate. After the last addition of sugar, scrape down the sides of the bowl and mix again briefly. Cover and place the bowl in the refrigerator for 30 minutes to thicken.

On a lightly floured work surface, roll the dough out to a thickness of ½ inch. Using a pastry cutter or a wide-mouth glass, cut the dough into circles, then incorporate the scraps after the first round. Pour the oil into a cast-iron Dutch oven or other deep, heavy-bottomed pot until it reaches a depth of 3 to 4 inches. Heat the oil over medium-high heat to 360°F. Fry the donuts and holes until golden brown on both sides, about 2 minutes. Remove with a slotted spoon and drain on wire racks. Let cool, then use a spatula to smear the frosting over the donuts. *Makes about 24 donuts*

Chefly Donuts

modern chefs now cast wistful eyes at donuts, intent upon reinventing the rounds in chefly ways. The appeals are many. Doughnuts wield a nostalgia wallop. Served at the close of a formal meal, they are irreverent, playful, an American riff on the French petits fours. And they are backed by precedent.

On November 6, 1940, United Press reported that Rupert Huba, a chef who was said to have distinguished himself in service to the Hapsburg court of Austria (where donuts known as *Faschingkrapfen* are suffused with, among other fillings, apricot preserves), had "lifted the doughnut out of the lower classes today—with a fork."

The result was Mr. Doughnut, the pre-dunked doughnut, "an aloof, if soggy, member of the sinker family. Its main characteristic is its sense of propriety—it takes its baths privately, untouched by human hands." The idea, said Huba, "struck me like the lightning.

"I am a chef in Hollywood," he said. "I bake the doughnuts. Lots of doughnuts. The stars, they order them, yes. But then they sit. They are unhappy. Their hands, they hover over the coffee cups, but no, they cannot dunk. Not in the public eye." While watching Hollywood royalty fret, Huba hatched his idea: "I think, 'Why should I not dunk the doughnut for them?' And then I do it. Mr. Doughnut, it is born."

To attain his ideal, Huba worked with a mechanic to devise a machine which—after the donuts (goosed with a pinch of coffee grounds) emerged from the fryer—lowered them into a shallow pan of coffee and slid them onto a plate. "The fork, she is the final touch," said Huba. "Eating the doughnut with a fork, that is class."

When überchef Thomas Keller of the French Laundry in Napa Valley, California, began serving his signature donuts-and-coffee dessert, he was likely unaware of the pioneering work of Rupert Huba. Keller was not so much concerned with class as he was American ingredients and ethos, reworked by way of French technique.

From this rubric came his macaroni and cheese, which paid tribute to the humdrum of the straight-from-the-box Kraft icon while suggesting that, with proper care and the best of ingredients, an everyman's dish was worthy of the damask tablecloth. It was an emboldening moment in American cooking, cemented, in 1999, by the publication of his fifty-dollar doorstop of a book, *The French Laundry Cookbook*.

The book made an unprecedented impact. It was one thing to eat at the French Laundry and report back to friends and colleagues the rigors and delights of a meal that might last three hours, proceeding from *amuse-bouche* (cornets of salmon tartare) to sweet (aforementioned cinnamon-sugar micro-donuts with cappuccino *semifreddo*), but it was another thing altogether to curl up on a couch with a catalogue of titillating recipes and color-saturated photographs and thumb

the pages at your leisure, like a twelve-year-old tracing the li-
bido of first love.

The French Laundry Cookbook became the chef's tome of the
new millennium, and, while it would be folly to credit Keller
as the sole catalyst for the trend, it's likely that his recipe,
right there on page 262, was the inspiration for many a donut
riff. In Keller's wake came co-conspirators.

At Craft, Tom Colicchio's mix-and-match New York restaurant, Karen DeMasco began dishing pyramids of cinnamon
sugar–dusted donuts with holes perched atop in the manner
of distended navels. On the side came sauces of caramel and
chocolate for dipping. Farther downtown, Lauren Dawson of
Hearth introduced apple cider donuts tasting faintly of buttermilk. After slicking them with an apple cider glaze, she spooned
applesauce on a plate and spritzed some whipped cream.

In New Orleans, the beignet was reborn in the hands of
pastry chefs like Joy Jessup of Rene Bistro. Her beignets came
goosed with Valrhona Caraïbe chocolate, nestled atop banana mousseline, crowned with praline ice cream, drizzled
with praline sauce. Not to be outdone, Dickie Brennan's
Palace Café rolled out Bananas Foster beignets, a tribute to
the dish his uncle first served in 1951 on Royal Street, while
Sona, out in Los Angeles, debuted peanut butter ganache
beignets, atop a pedestal of rum-caramelized bananas, beneath a ball of bitter caramel ice cream.

From what I can tell, the trend knows no geographical or
ideological bounds. At various times within the past couple of
years, Azure in Boston was serving gingerbread donuts with
pear soup; Andalu in San Francisco was offering donut holes

with Castilian hot chocolate for dipping; and Hugo's in Houston was frying long churro twigs and serving them with Mexican hot chocolate.

With any luck, those restaurants will still be serving donuts when next I visit. I mention luck because I fear the craze may be a prolonged flirt instead of a long-term commitment on the part of America's pastry chefs. Of course, I may be wrong. Keller, for his part, is holding up his end of the bargain. Last time I was in Napa, his Bouchon Bakery—a couple of blocks south of the French Laundry—was serving its own donuts.

Alongside blood-orange tarts, in sight of featherweight croissants and madeleines, there rose a three-tiered platter stacked with poufs of dough, some stuffed with ganache and pocked with chocolate pearls, others dusted with cinnamon sugar and filled with vanilla cream. These were good, in their own way, but they paled in comparison to the lemon curd lovelies perched, appropriately enough, at the top. Powdered with confectioners' sugar and piped with a mixture that was at once tart and sweet, luxe and demure, they required no fork to stake a claim to class—and to posterity.

new
traditionalists

everything changed when Krispy Kreme escaped the southern provinces. Donuts were, all of a sudden, à la mode. Rosie O'Donnell was singing about them on her talk show. Bill Clinton was receiving boxes at the White House. Dick Clark, the ultimate arbiter of hipness, signed on as a franchisee, joining Jimmy Buffett and Hank Aaron.

Fortune, in a July 2003 story, declared Krispy Kreme to be "the hottest brand in America." And after a fifty-plus-year drought, *The New Yorker* deigned the marginalized donut coverage, engaging the talents of Nora Ephron, who declared the original glazed to be "light as a frosted snowflake" and described the Manhattan beachhead as a "shrine, complete with pilgrims, fanatics, converts, and proselytizers—the sort of religious experience New Yorkers like me are far more receptive to than the ones that actually involve God."

The Krispy Kreme wedding cake phenomenon seems to have hit its zenith in 2002, about the same time the bed-head movie-star-in-a-trucker-cap look was au courant. Although I saw photographs of many, I saw only one in the flesh, as it were. I was in Manhattan, walking an Upper East Side avenue. And there it was, in the window of a jewelry store, or maybe it was a stationer's—a four-foot-tall tier of original glazed, draped in lilac ribbons, festooned with strands of pearls, garnished with garnet-throated parrot tulips.

Krispy Kreme wedding cakes are no longer A-list. If they ever were. And yet, out of this short-lived fervor for straight-out-of-Winston-Salem flavor has come a new generation of donut makers. They see Krispy Kreme as a business model worthy of replication, not a gastronomic ideal worthy of supplication. I call them, for lack of a better descriptor, New Traditionalists.

ELEVEN

Donuts in Bloom

either Mark Isreal, proprietor of the Doughnut Plant, a raw steel–framed pastry gallery on the Lower East Side of Manhattan, dwells upon an astral plane where streets are bricked with chocolate bars and powdered sugar falls like snow on winter nights, or he's stoned 24/7. For the longest time, I couldn't figure out which.

Standing in front of his store on a spring day in 2004, I think back over previous visits, trying to makes sense of the scene. In years past, each time I stopped by his shop, he emerged, squinty-eyed, from the back with a story of sacrifice and sleeplessness. I recall him as always just shy of hysterical. But times have changed.

"I spent three years in the basement, just me and the dough," Isreal told me in September of 2002, when we first met and I first had the chance to scarf a couple glazed with the juice of fresh-squeezed Valencias. "It wasn't easy. I spent a lot of nights crying into my dough. I still get sad when I think about serving a donut that has wilted. I want everyone to taste my donuts when they're blooming, when they're fresh."

At the time, I was not confident of my ability to discern the difference between blooming and wilting donuts. In fact, I still consider myself a novice. But, then as now, I can vouch for the ethereal texture and taste of Isreal's product. And so, each time I traveled to New York, I returned to his doorstep.

In November of that same year, roasted-chestnut donuts were the flavor of the moment and Isreal, a lummox of a guy who binds his coif in a do-rag, was flipping through an old Rolodex, thinking of those years in the basement. "I used to write notes to myself so that I would remember," he told me, in the manner of a shell-shocked war veteran. "Here's one: 'Never forget the pain. Mixer broke. Three months behind on rent.' And another: 'My whole body is so sore and I'm in so much pain . . . Never forget how hard it was.'"

Six months later, on a humid summer morning, I ate a yeast donut pocked with blueberry bits as Mark waxed philosophical. "Krispy Kreme is about dough stabilizers and conditioners," he said. "They use bleached flour. They do that to take control of the dough. I let the dough speak. My dough is natural. It's alive. My mood affects it. The weather affects it. Like apples on a tree, each dough is different. I'm about artisanship, about working my craft so that the dough reveals its potential. Anything else wouldn't be honest. People who eat my donuts can feel the energy I put into them. They can taste the devotion."

———

Soon after Mark told me this, I embraced my cynical tendencies. Though still fond of Mark's donuts, I grew suspect of his shtick. I knew Mark wasn't a stoner. But I wasn't so sure he was genuine.

Of course, Mark still emerged from the back to say hello when I called, but he was usually too busy to talk. One time I spied him through the porthole windows that frame the prep room. Mark was walking back and forth, from dough table to fryer, trailed by a clutch of Japanese businessmen. When he stuck his head around the corner to tell me about developing rose petal donuts for Valentine's Day, the men crumpled into his backside like Keystone Kops. "We're opening a Doughnut Plant in Japan," Mark told me. And then he and his daisy chain were gone.

By this point, the whole tortured-genius-with-his-head-in-a-cumulus-of-flour act was wearing thin. How could an artisan with a preternatural affection for living, breathing dough take his show on the road to Tokyo? What would happen to the dough he left behind? Wouldn't it grow lonely? Wouldn't it, like its master, suffer? Would the savor be absent, the taste of devotion lost?

but that was then. This is now. Maybe Mark sensed my skepticism. Maybe I willed the transformation. But on this spring day, when I return to the shop to buy a dozen for the trip home from New York, he drops the shtick and tells his story by way of his grandfather's. In the telling, I hear a tale that reveals more about his life and his donuts than any tear-soaked *Like Water for Chocolate* pabulum could.

I sit on a bench, embedded in a rainbow assemblage of ceramic donuts made by his sculptor father, as Mark tells me of his grandfather, Herman Isreal. Born in Tennessee of Finnish parents, he settled in Greensboro, North Carolina, where he ran the College Pastry Shop. Donuts were but one of his specialties. "He died in 1966, when I was three," Mark says, twisting a silver dollar ring that I later learn was Herman's. "I never really knew him, I don't think, until I came across his donut recipe."

Finding Greensboro limiting, provincial, Mark had made his way to New York at the age of sixteen. In time he found work, first as a busboy at Studio 54, the church of disco culture, later as a bartender at CBGB, the citadel of punk rock. The donut epiphany came a few years later.

"I was home visiting," Mark recalls. "My father had come across my grandfather's old file boxes. It was a rainy day, and we were looking through the files when I found this donut recipe and thought, 'Well, we don't have anything to do.' We went through pounds and pounds of flour that day. I couldn't believe I could make something so good."

From there, Mark's tale builds quickly. "The idea was totally spontaneous," he recalls. "I went to this coffee shop in my building, down on Avenue A, and asked them something like, 'If I made some donuts, would you sell them?' That was back in 1994. I'm not sure why they said yes. But I went home and started making donuts."

And so began the saga of nights spent working in a onetime boiler room, crying into his dough, mornings spent pedaling his bike through the streets, delivering pistachio-glazed and orange-glazed organic treats to coffee shops and gourmet grocers. Fame came fairly quickly, for Mark's donuts were different. These donuts did not collapse beneath bicuspids. In the manner of loafs of peasant bread, they offered a hint of resistance; they required the slightest tug. Whereas most yeast donuts were textureless, Mark's were substantial. Until I tasted my first Doughnut Plant product, I believed the terms "donut" and "texture" to be mutually exclusive, thinking all the while about George Carlin's riff on jumbo shrimp and military intelligence.

Sure, by the time I first showed up, Mark was already at the top of his game. Maybe he was even growing egotistical. He had spent time in Oaxaca, Mexico, and returned with a recipe for an idealized churro. When the World Series came to town, he debuted a blueberry pinstripe donut in honor of the Yankees. In advance of Chinese New Year, he crafted a fresh ginger donut. And the press came calling, clamoring, yelping. *New York* magazine shot gooey close-ups. Emeril brought his crew. Martha came and went. And Mark proved a quick study, honing his tears-in-the-dough story into the perfect thirty-second sound bite.

Now Tokyo is calling. Five locations are in the offing. Mark no longer seems on the verge of hysterics. He's calm, measured, assured. And his donuts are as good as ever, if the banana cream–filled peanut butter–glazed Elvis tribute donut I just finished is any indication.

I kind of miss the off-kilter Mark. But I don't begrudge his

transformation from oddball to mogul. No, on this spring afternoon, as Mark's donuts bloom and my appetite for them
proves voracious, I will eat my fill and imagine a future when
my cynicism no longer haunts me and Mark's donuts are always within easy reach.

Two Doughnut Plant–Inspired Glazes

Getting a donut recipe out of Mark Isreal is impossible. He thinks of recipes as a kind of family dowry. And he should. But I figured his glazes would be another matter. Instead of asking Mark for glaze recipes, I ask him about glaze strategies, about how to get a liquid to drape a donut in a mantle of sugary sheen. But he's not willing to go there either. So, using Nancy Silverton's Pastries from the La Brea Bakery *as guide, I came up with two glazes for yeast-raised donuts. Forgive me, Mark, it's the best I could do.*

GOLD LEAF GLAZE

- ½ cup confectioners' sugar
- ¼ cup heavy cream
- Dash of vanilla extract
- Dash of salt
- Edible gold leaf (available from bakers' supply houses)

Heat 2 cups of water to a simmer in the bottom of a double boiler. In the top of the double boiler, combine the confectioners' sugar, heavy cream, vanilla, and salt. Heat until warm, stirring constantly. Remove

(continued)

from the heat and let the glaze cool for about 10 minutes before dunking your donuts in the glaze. Scatter gold leaf over the glaze, working to ensure a lapped coating. If the gold leaf is difficult to lift without tearing, try rubbing a pastry brush over the back of your hand to create static and then rub it lightly over the gold leaf sheet to allow the static to lift the sheet. The gold will stick to the brush and then you can use the brush to gently lay the gold leaf onto the donut.

PISTACHIO GLAZE

- ½ cup confectioners' sugar
- ¼ cup heavy cream
- Dash of amaretto
- Dash of salt
- ¼ cup shelled pistachios

Heat 2 cups of water to a simmer in the bottom of a double boiler. In the top of the double boiler, combine the confectioners' sugar, heavy cream, amaretto, and salt. Heat until warm, stirring constantly. Remove from the heat. Using the heel of a heavy pot or skillet, crush half of the pistachios and toss in the liquid. Add the remainder and stir to combine. Let the glaze cool for about 10 minutes before dunking your donuts in the glaze.

TWELVE

Tip Top

top Pot Doughnuts, set in a greenhouse moderne building in the shadow of the Seattle monorail line, is a traffic-
stopper. Out front, a bling-bling neon sign with a bucking
bronco rider heralds an enterprise of the Willie Wonka
School. Just this morning, while perusing the newspaper, I
learned the sign comes with a good story: Rescued from the
Top Spot, a derelict Chinese restaurant in the Rainier Valley,
it lost the S when it fell off the truck as brothers Mark and
Mike Klebeck ferried it home to Seattle. The culprit was, if I
recall correctly, a band of raccoons who, while making their
home in the sign, chewed through the guy wires that kept the
letter in place.

Damn cute story aside, I'm not keen on the interior. It's a bit
reserved. Maybe the word is "uptight." I wouldn't use the term

"avant-conservative," but I could make a good case for using such a conjunction, what with the techno-squawk music playing on the stereo and the two-story floor-to-ceiling bookshelves stocked with leather-bound editions of, among other books, Ayn Rand's oeuvre. The blond wood, the Heywood-Wakefield chairs, the vintage automobile upholstery, the whole designed-within-an-inch-of-its-life loft look fosters a mood that is, depending upon your donut aesthetic, either fey and affected or a welcome escape from the boomerang Formica norm.

You could argue with some success that I shouldn't be so tough on the brothers Klebeck, for they come by their hipness honestly. Mike is the mechanic, the guy who keeps the dough sheeters working. Mark, a buzz-cut blond, is a surf rocker turned front-of-the-house man. More specifically, when he's not peddling donuts, he's a guitar player in a band called the Kings of Hawaii. And he's no poseur. A few years back, his band opened on a tour with El Vez, the Mexican Elvis, singer of such standards as "En el Barrio" and "Immigration Time," the latter of which is sung to the tune of "Suspicious Minds."

By the time I cross their threshold, the brothers Klebeck have already conquered coffee. In the city where Starbucks was born, where drive-thru espresso stands seem as omnipresent as drive-thru McDonald's, they have earned a citywide rep for fine, herbaceous brews. "Donuts seemed like the next step," Mark tells me as he sips a coffee and I demolish a chocolate donut glazed with chocolate icing, known in Top Pot speak as a Double Trouble. "Seattle had been through this scone phase. But I always thought people would come around to something that was better, cheaper."

before the Klebecks hit upon donuts, they pondered opening a hemp clothing store. But that was a bit *too* hip, even for the brothers. "We started working on this before Krispy Kreme came to Iassaquah," Mark says, referring to the 2001 Krispy Kreme opening in the Seattle suburbs that set what was then a company record of more than $400,000 in first-week sales. "But you can't deny the impact of their brand. They created the hype. In much the same way that Starbucks gave everybody the go-ahead to pay three dollars for a cup of coffee, Krispy Kreme proved that donuts mattered again."

The brothers Klebeck are earnest, forthright. Their knack for naming donuts—Feather Boas for pink-icing-haloed cake donuts with a flutter of coconut, Valley Girl Lemon for yeast donuts stuffed with "tart" jelly—notwithstanding, they approach the endeavor like technicians.

"A lot of people have childhood donut memories," says Mark. "We grew up going to St. Francis Cabrini in Tacoma. After the nine-thirty service, we went to the House of Doughnuts to eat what I remember as these huge, raised donuts." A two-beat pause and a sip of espresso follow this last statement. Mark searches for the right words. He frowns. He looks over my shoulder at the pastry case, stocked with pyramids of donuts, stacked on antique silver chargers of the type a wealthy great aunt might flourish on Thanksgiving. "The thing is, what we do today is informed by that childhood experience," he says, summoning a bit of gravitas. "But it's not limited by that."

The brothers have big plans. They see a sweet spot, ripe for expansion, in the chasm that separates the commodified nostalgia of Krispy Kreme and the artisanal approach of the Doughnut Plant. "We spent a lot of time experimenting with home recipes," says Mark. "And we probably spent an equal amount of time toying with commercial mixes. It was trial and error. We tried different proofing times, different temperatures. In the end, we went with an unorthodox oil solution. That's our secret weapon."

If Mark sounds like an entrepreneur set upon expansion, that's because he is. "We've got our own label of mix now," he says. "It's better than the stuff you can buy off the truck. It's not intended for the one-guy-and-a-rolling-pin market. But he could use it and make a good donut. We want to straddle both worlds. We don't cook our donuts on conveyor belt machines. Our cake donuts are hand extruded. Our yeast donuts are hand cut. We look at what's out there and we see possibilities."

even before the soliloquy, I was sold. And so, over the course of a week spent in and around Seattle, I stop off the Top Pot flagship store every morning, intent upon working my way through the sushi-style check-off menu. On Monday, I scarf a raspberry chocolate cake. On Tuesday, I lick my fingers clean of chocolate rainbow icing. On Wednesday, I return to roots with a nutmeg cake. Every time I inquire about whether Mark is around, I learn that he was up late into the night, working with the bakers, making needed adjustments to the process. He's expected in soon, I'm always told.

On my next-to-the-last day in town, I find Mark. I've just finished a plain cake. Mark is sitting at a table on the store's mezzanine level, turning a saucer over and over again in his hands. It's one of those heavy china saucers, the seemingly indestructible stuff made famous by the Buffalo China Company.

This one is a dull white color. Along the rim is a faint gray stripe. And bisecting that line is a decidedly retro logo featuring two young men with matching toques, their heads touching, temple to temple in a kind of Siamese twin pose. In the center, obscuring the left eye of one and the right eye of the other, is an oversized donut. The net effect seems to be that the two men share tunnel vision. Or donut vision. Or something like that.

If I had not seen the logo somewhere before, I would have thought it the perfect mark for the brothers Klebeck. But I had seen it before. The question of where, however, stumps me. I ask Mark. He smiles. "This is an old saucer," he says, handing it to me. "The logo was used by the Doughnut Corporation of America a long while back. We saw it and liked it and did a little digging. We eventually went through a trademark lawyer. He found out it had been abandoned thirty or forty years ago. So we bought the logo and the name, hoping it might come in handy someday."

Pink Feather Boas

■ 1 recipe Zingerman's Roadhouse Donuts
(page 164; omit the final sprinkling of
muscovado sugar)

FROSTING
■ ½ cup (1 stick) unsalted butter, softened
■ Dash of coconut liqueur
■ 3 cups confectioners' sugar
■ 3 tablespoons heavy cream
■ Dash of red food coloring

In a large bowl, working with an electric mixer, cream
the butter with the coconut liqueur. Gradually add
the confectioners' sugar, mixing well after each addition. Scrape down the sides of the bowl after the final
addition of sugar, and add the heavy cream and food
coloring. Scrape the bowl again, and mix briefly, until
all of the color is incorporated. Cover and place the
bowl in the refrigerator for 30 minutes to thicken. Using a spatula, smear the glaze on the cooled donuts.
Makes 24 donuts

Spudnuts and Churros

mark Isreal and the brothers Klebeck are smart businessmen. But the chance that one of their companies breaks out of the pack to become the next big thing
seems slight, for the world of franchised donuts is mercurial.
Personality-driven enterprises are difficult to replicate. Per-
fection is nigh-impossible to clone. And consumers sense the
loss, the small defeats that define a transition from hands-on
training to handing over an employee manual.

Aim a little lower, say the handicappers, fix upon a more
modest trajectory; that's what Krispy Kreme did. And the handicappers are right. Wipe away the glaze and you'll discover that
Krispy Kreme did nothing more—and nothing less—than revi-
talize a brand. They didn't tinker with the formula. They didn't
launch a new product. Krispy Kreme merely dusted off a retro
logo and set up shop in districts where their goods were novel.

With the right marketing plan and a strong infusion of
cash, Spudnuts could be next. The brand isn't exactly
moribund. There are at least a couple Spudnuts in Los Angeles. The Richland, Washington, location just celebrated
fifty years in business. In El Dorado, Arkansas, Spudnuts is
the community clubhouse for the cane-and-walker set. In

Charlottesville, Virginia, Spudnuts is an after-hours destination for college students with a snootful.

I've heard rumors of a Spudnuts museum in Lafayette, Indiana, but I've been unable to gain admission. Truth is, I've been unable to determine whether the museum exists. But I keep hope alive, for I'm thinking that the curator of such a museum would be in a position to tell me whether the TatoNut Shop down in Ocean Springs, Mississippi, is, as I suspect, a renegade Spudnuts, long gone native.

Spudnuts has the backstory around which a brand can be built. As the name suggests, potato flour is one of the primary ingredients. That harkens to the traditional cookery of a number of ethnic groups, including the Pennsylvania Dutch, who have long doted on fried morning cakes made with last night's mashed potatoes. And the potato flour links Spudnuts to Krispy Kreme, which, although the corporation is hush-hush about such matters today, tipped its hat to its secrets in newspaper advertisements of the early 1950s, proclaiming their donuts to be "chock-full of ingredients with high nutritional value" like "eggs, milk, [and] potatoes."

The goofiness of the name helps, too; Spudnuts sounds like an improbable moniker for a commercial concern with national aspirations. In the counterintuitive world of donuts, that's a boon. Now if a band of Spudnuts owners could just pull together a marketing consortium, they'd be halfway home. A gimmick might help. I always thought that Dunkin' Donuts made a huge mistake when they jettisoned their trademark cake, the one with the built-in handle. Maybe that's a place to start.

the Venezuelan company behind Churromania has already settled on its shtick. And it appears to have money and marketing acumen. With more than forty locations throughout the Spanish-speaking world, they are the lead dog in a hunt that includes competing franchisors like Mr. Churro U.S.A. and freezer case suppliers like Tio Pepe's, which cross-promotes their treats to Anglos as "waffle sticks."

On a trip to Miami, I stop off at the Dolphin Mall location of Churromania. Over the course of the previous year, I had become aware of America's budding passion for churros. My pal Robb Walsh over in Houston had been raving about the churros with hot chocolate at Hugo's, his city's temple of haute Mexican cookery. I had heard good things about the churros with mescal cream dished by Scott Linquist, chef at Dos Caminos SoHo in New York.

I had read, with interest, reports of passage of California Assembly Bill 1045, which decreed churro vendors to be unfettered by health code regulations against cooking foods on the street. Somebody in the California state house knows that a cold churro—like a cold donut—is but a ghost.

And I had eaten my fill of churros at walk-up stands in Los Angeles and Miami, watching as men and women loaded cylinders of *masa de churro* into Catherine wheel devices that, when cranked, extruded thin streams of ridged dough into cauldrons of burbling oil. Haute cuisine riffs notwithstanding, those streetside churros were the standard by which I judged all others—until I glimpsed the world imagined by Churromania.

The Dolphin Mall franchise, like the others, is a wonderland of kinetic colors and what an industry type might call churro platform foods. I step to the counter, reading the backlit menu board as I go, trying to discern the differences between the registered trademark treats known as Crispy Mania, Big Mania, Glazed Mania, Twist Mania, and Churromania.

I fail, and, unable to decipher the differences by way of communication with the clerk who—in the time-honored manner of all fast-food clerks—appears more focused upon escape than assistance, order one of each. Turns out that there are really two products: skinny churros (dusted with sugar or drizzled with a variety of toppings, including *dulce de leche* and strawberry) and fat churros (filled with your choice of the aforementioned toppings and, if you like, saddled in whipped cream).

Seated on a bench facing the promenade that bisects the mall, I balance cardboard trays of various Mania on each knee and ponder the future. By the time you read this, Churromania may well have opened a location in your local megamall. (As of 2005, it had seven spots in Florida.) Already there are whispers in the Hispanic community that they are to be the Hispanic Krispy Kreme. But the men and women behind the brand have bigger plans. They know that a love of fried dough translates into any tongue.

the
future

i met Jim Beatty, better known as Jimmy Doughnuts, when I was putting this book to bed. It was September of 2005. The first round of edits was finished. I was polishing here, cutting there. But I was still looking, still tasting.

A Chicago native, Beatty had begun selling donuts from a cart in downtown Louisville, Kentucky, that summer. I learned, as I nibbled at one of his glazed cakes, that he is a cancer survivor who, when his doctor told him to eat whatever he wanted, chose donuts. As remission followed recovery, Beatty transitioned from working in advertising to working in dough. And when his wife took a job in Louisville, he brought his passion south, setting up a canteen and a cart for cooking and peddling.

Beatty claims to fry and sell "the best tasting donuts on earth." For now, he makes the best donuts in Louisville. And that might be enough. His customers in Louisville love him. So do the ones Beatty left behind in Chicago, where the following dispatch—a glimpse into the future of food in general and donuts in particular—reveals a gastronomic idealism that may prove ephemeral.

For now, Jimmy Doughnuts stays the course. And talk of change, of expansion, is limited to Beatty's roster of glazes. Lemon-lavender is on the horizon. Strawberry-thyme may follow. Donut soup is, for now, beyond the ken.

THIRTEEN

A.D.D. Central

hey're eating air!" says Kim, my dining companion, gesturing toward the next table. "I'm serious, they're eating air!" I swivel a bit to gain better peripheral vantage. At this dinner, anything is possible. Alongside, a slouchy guy and a sylph of a girl, their faces registering more doubt than delight, stare at red balloons that are, of their own seeming volition, inflating.

The girl prods, unsure whether she should use a fork or call Homeland Security. After a moment, the balloons burst and the guy and girl take long pulls from their wineglasses before reaching for fortune cookie–style slips of paper that flutter to their plates. I lean over, curious. "The chef was just welcoming us back," the guy says. "It's been a while."

Every child knows the sorrow of watching a balloon deflate. But at Moto, chef Homaro Cantu's new restaurant in Chicago's meat-packing district, the implicit promise is that a second childhood, during which balloons are forever inflating and lobster comes in a sauce of Orange Crush, is not only achievable, it's imminent, due to arrive sometime between the sushi cartoon and the donut soup.

designed with a minimalist's palate and executed with a maximalist's pretensions, Moto has staked a tentative claim as the enfant terrible of the Chicago restaurant scene. It's a moniker that Cantu, a veteran of four years as sous chef at Charlie Trotter's eponymous temple of gastronomy, appears to wear with pride. He should; competition for the title is stiff.

Yet Moto, known to serve prosciutto cotton candy with pear soup, and fried salad with brûléed utensils, stands apart. There are any number of likely reasons for this. You might argue that twenty-nine-year-old Cantu's fondness for space-age tinkering was born of his father's employ as an engineer. Or, staring down at edible literature of explorateur with hundred-year-old *balsamico,* you might decide that Cantu booked Coleridge's passage to Kubla Khan.

But earlier that day, when I visited his subterranean kitchen, as Cantu and pastry chef Ben Roche were deconstructing donuts, I got a glimpse of something different. I hesitate to term it "hubris," though Cantu's sometimes errant ego informs all, as in when I asked whether a diner might add a dish from the eighteen-course *grand tour Moto* to the ten-course menu. "You wouldn't go to the opera and order act four," he told me. "It just doesn't work that way." I got an inkling of the same when I asked about the restaurant's back-of-town location, on a street populated by hot dog wholesalers. "I don't want foot traffic," Cantu told me. "I want this to be a place of pilgrimage."

A better label might be naiveté, for the best of his cooking—say french fry potato chain links with sweet potato pie or the aforementioned lobster with freshly squeezed orange soda—showcases a boyish exuberance that is undeniably infectious. Put another way, Cantu seems to be in possession of all of his chefly faculties but, in the manner of a teenager driving his father's new 7 Series BMW, has yet to grasp the power beckoned by applying his foot to the pedal.

Although Cantu probably would not warm to my analysis, I can't think of a better way to characterize a man who, when I asked about what's next, said, "This place is A.D.D. central," and ceded the floor to Roche, who began demonstrating his newest creation, a donut-shaped alginate polymer filled with coffee, and talking of his next. "I'm thinking about veal donuts," said Roche. "Maybe a chain-link dish of donuts and sausages."

back at our table, myriad courses have come and gone since the balloon ascent. Some, like sushi cartoon, a cylinder of soybean paper filled with vinegared rice and imprinted with ghostly images of various nori, were oddly satisfying. Ditto the monkfish with smoked olive broth; served in a steamer box, the dish perfumed our table with an aroma that reminded me of the best bottle of Chinon I ever drank. Others, say French onion soup with a hot-frozen crouton, were just plain odd.

But our evening was not absent the sublime. The lobster with freshly squeezed soda was, by everyone's measure, a delight. The dish arrived at table as two square bowls, one with perfectly poached lobster meat and brown butter ice cream, another with a half orange, which, thanks to an injection of carbon dioxide, became orange soda when squeezed. And although I was disappointed that the braised pizza was nothing more than stewed greens bound by red sauce and cheese, I loved the oversized fork and spoon that flanked the dish. Were it not for the cloves of garlic speared on the apex of each, I would have thought them to be shock absorbers liberated from a minibike.

Later, I will tell a friend that our dinner was a ten-course punch line. And I will confess that the joke was that we spent five hours listening. Of course, such summary judgment as that isn't fair; Cantu is a chef emboldened by both talent and bravura. But it does give some indication of my mood upon exiting the restaurant, snacking on what I came to call salt-and-pepper Styrofoam with caramel soup.

The best judge of any restaurant is whether you would hasten to return. In the case of Moto, once is enough. Sure, that could have something to do with my tab, which inclusive of wine and tip, was $375 for two. More important, I make such a judgment fully aware that, if I never cross Moto's threshold again, I may never again taste course nine, the apotheosis of all childhood dreams, donut soup—which translates on the palate as puréed essence of Krispy Kreme.

But with that ethereal taste top of mind, I'm hedging my bets. You see, during the time I spent down in the basement at Ben Roche's side, he shared one of the secrets to making his signature demitasse of donut. The recipe I offer below is not his, but until you book passage to Chicago for a one-in-lifetime Moto pilgrimage, it will have to suffice.

Donut Soup

- 2 cups whole milk
- 1 tablespoon unsalted butter
- 2 glazed yeast donuts

Pour the milk into a blender and set aside. Melt the butter in a medium sauté pan over medium-high heat. When the butter foams, add the donuts and cook on each side for a minute or two until the glaze caramelizes. Toss the donuts into the milk and let them soak for 30 minutes, then purée until smooth. Pour the soup into a saucepan and heat until just shy of a simmer. Serve in demitasse cups alongside cups of espresso. *Serves 6*

An Epiphany,
a Recipe,
a Primer

An Epiphany

I was reared on yeast-raised donuts. If I was lucky, I ate them hot off the conveyor belt at the Krispy Kreme factory in Macon, twelve miles south of my hometown, Clinton, Georgia. If I was unlucky, I mooched a couple while walking door-to-door on a humid summer afternoon, selling boxes of twelve to benefit our Little League Baseball team's travel fund. They were constants of my childhood. When I was eleven, I snuck Krispy Kremes into a *Planet of the Apes* movie marathon and ate every morsel during the previews. When I was thirteen and distraught over a four-interception performance as quarterback of my Midget League Football team, I wallowed in the false succor of a half-dozen glazed.

When I was nineteen, I took a summer job peddling encyclopedias in Washington state. Equipped with a satchel full of samples, I walked the working-class neighborhoods of Olympia. I was a dissolute failure. I didn't sell books. I didn't learn school-of-hard-knocks lessons. Instead, I spent much of that two-month stretch cowered in a donut shop, thumbing sticky fingers through my samples, sipping lukewarm coffee. One good thing came to pass during that chilly summer: I learned to love cake donuts. I came to appreciate the comparative restraint of a brown round spiked with a bit of nutmeg. Most important, in the manner of a Wonder Bread boy facing down his first sourdough *bâtard*, I savored texture, which—let's be honest here—I never knew during my Krispy Kreme–fueled childhood.

In the ensuing couple decades, my horizons widened. My tastes became catholic. Put another way, while researching this book I did not seek donuts of a particular camp. Yeast or cake structure, rice or wheat flour, Italian or Dutch origin, it mattered not a whit. I sought donuts that told me a story of America. And the tales surfaced quickly, came easily.

the donut makers, on the other hand, proved more difficult. They are a welcoming lot. They hand out free samples. They talk a good game. But, for the most part, they are vague on the subject of technique. For those who rely upon commercial mixes, there's really not much to tell: Slit open a bag of dry ingredients. Add a liquid. Stir into a dough. Proof, if necessary. Roll out, cut rounds, and fry. The decided minority, who make their donuts from scratch, cracking eggs, sifting flour, grating nutmeg, have a lot to tell. But they are less inclined to talk.

Sure, I read a host of books on the subject. Among the best is *Fearless Frying* by John Martin Taylor, with eleven variations on the fritter/donut theme, including a knock-you-in-the-ditch fig beignet courtesy of Madeleine Kamman. And as with all donut matters, the works of Sally Levitt Steinberg, most especially *The Donut Book,* proved a boon. But I didn't truly get a handle on how to cook donuts at home until I spent a morning in the kitchen at Zingerman's Roadhouse, an offshoot of the world-renowned Ann Arbor, Michigan–based specialty foods retailer.

Under the tutelage of chef Alex Young, and with the input of fesser Ari Weinzweig, I learn the ways and means of the cake donut. I am changed. After forty-odd years in the wilderness, I find my way home. The recipe, inspired by a Dutch donut in Steinberg's book, refined by perusing the *Joy of Cooking* as well as Bill and Cheryl Jamison's *A Real American Breakfast,* is reprinted below, tendered by the boys at Zingerman's, annotated by me. For those who have never attempted a donut at home, it's the perfect place to start. For those who consider themselves experienced but aspire to better donuts, consider this an instruction in the apotheosis of the form.

A Recipe

Zingerman's Roadhouse Donuts

- 5 cups all-purpose flour
- 1 tablespoon baking powder
- 2 teaspoons freshly grated nutmeg
- 1½ teaspoons salt
- ½ cup buttermilk, at room temperature
- 2 large eggs, at room temperature
- 1 large egg yolk, at room temperature
- ¾ cup granulated sugar
- ½ cup vegetable shortening, melted and cooled
- ¼ cup molasses
- ½ rounded teaspoon lemon zest
- ½ gallon vegetable oil for frying
- ½ cup muscovado brown sugar for sprinkling (or substitute dark brown sugar)

Sift the flour, baking powder, nutmeg, and salt together into a large mixing bowl. In another large mixing bowl, combine the buttermilk, eggs, egg yolk, granulated sugar, melted vegetable shortening, molasses, and lemon zest.

Gradually add the flour mixture to the wet mixture, stirring gently. Stop stirring as soon as all the ingredients are combined—overstirring will make tough doughnuts. You'll still see a little flour. (You may use a standing mixer for this process—just be sure to stop mixing as soon as all the flour is added and combined.) Cover the dough with plastic and let rest in the refrigerator for at least 1 hour.

Pour the oil into a cast-iron Dutch oven or other heavy-bottomed and deep pot until it reaches a depth of 3 to 4 inches. Heat the oil over medium-high heat to 370°F.

Knead the dough on a well-floured surface for 1 minute, then roll it out with a rolling pin to ½ inch thickness. Cut out rounds using a 3½ inch pastry cutter, then cut the centers out with a 1½ inch round. Gather the scraps and reroll as necessary.

To avoid overcrowding, fry only 2 or 3 donuts at a time. All told, they'll take about 3 to 4 minutes to cook, needing to be turned every minute or so. Drop the rings into the hot oil. They will float in about 30 seconds or so. Fry them 1 minute more, then turn them over and fry for another minute. Turn them once again and fry 1 minute more, until golden. Remove

(continued)

with a slotted spoon onto a kitchen towel and immediately sprinkle with muscovado sugar. Cover the donuts
as you make them and store them in a warm place until they're all done. *Makes 30 donuts*

Even this recipe, with its sure language and exacting mea-
surements, doesn't tell you all you need to know. Among the
gleanings likely to be missed, unless you give it a go and then
try it again, is how the muscovado sugar sprinkled over the
top plays nicely off the dank sweetness of the molasses and
the back-of-the-throat kick of freshly ground nutmeg.

What's more, there's no mention of what to do with left-
overs which, one assumes, are few. First thing you should
know is that these donuts are worth eating a full day after you
fry them. But if you must fiddle with a Zingerman's donut on
day two, use it as the base of a sundae, like the Ann Arbor
boys do.

A Primer

EQUIPMENT AND COOKING MEDIUM

Start with a heavy kettle of at least a five-quart capacity. Fill it three to four inches deep with peanut oil, or a similar oil with a high smoke point. And in an effort to keep the temperature steady, invest in a candy thermometer of the type that will fix on the side.

GLAZES

Glazes are, in the words of an acquaintance with a knack for coinage, stupid simple. Mix a couple tablespoons of whole milk in a cup of confectioners' sugar, and you have enough stupid simple glaze for a couple dozen. Substitute a table-spoon of fruit juice—lemon, orange, cherry—and the input is no more difficult, while the output is leaps and bounds bet-ter than most icings from the corner shop. Add three or four tablespoons of powdered cocoa and half as much milk and you have a chocolate glaze.

FILLINGS

Take a pint of raspberries. De-stem, wash, purée, and strain. And there you have the filling for a jelly donut. Simpler still, spoon it from a jar put up by artisans, say, the strawberry jam from American Spoon Foods.

MIXES

In addition to the recipes appended to each chapter and the Zingerman's cake lovelies detailed here, there are, of course, more expedient means of making donuts. Among the best and most widely available mixes is sold by Café Du Monde of New Orleans. It's not bad, really, especially on those bleary-eyed mornings when you can't muster the energy to create your own mix. If you order a box by way of their Internet store at www.cafedumonde.com, you might as well get a tin of chicory coffee too.

REVIVIFICATION

Not all donuts have the staying power of Zingerman's cake donuts. Yeast donuts lose their bloom in a few hours. To vivify a stale yeast donut, a three-second blast in the Radar Range does wonders. Or you may try the old grease jockey's trick: Toss a pat of butter in a skillet or on a flattop set to medium high. When the butter melts, toss a glazed donut in the puddle and cook, flipping once, to a color just this side of caramel. Serve, as they do at the White Spot in Charlottesville, Virginia, and the Yankee Doodle in New Haven, Connecticut, with a scoop of ice cream in the center. The Doodle calls their confections Griddled Donuts; the Spot goes for the more enigmatic Grills With, suggesting the possibility of other embellishments.

Appendix

Black Book of Donut Shops

NORTHEAST

Butler's Colonial Doughnut
    House
459 Sanford Road
Westport, Massachusetts
508-672-4600

Dos Caminos SoHo
475 West Broadway
New York, New York
212-277-4300

Doughboy Police Supply
187 Summer Street
Kingston, Massachusetts
781-585-3000

Doughnut Plant
379 Grand Street
New York, New York
212-505-3700

Iggy's Doughboys and
    Chowder House
899 Oakland Beach
    Avenue
Warwick, Rhode Island
401-737-9459

Pastryland
417 Harvard Street
Brookline,
    Massachusetts
617-278-2400

SOUTHEAST

Café Du Monde
800 Decatur Street
New Orleans, Louisiana
504-525-4544

Churromania
11401 N.W. 12th Street
Miami, Florida
305-418-9050

Elizabeth's Restaurant
601 Gallier Street
New Orleans, Louisiana
504-944-9272

Fay's Take-Out and Honey
    Whip
801 Kepler Street
Gretna, Louisiana
504-366-9077

Hugo's
1602 Westheimer Road
Houston, Texas
713-524-7744

Jimmy Doughnuts
Jefferson Avenue, between
    5th and 6th Streets
Louisville, Kentucky
502-295-1962

Mulligan's
630 E. Lake Drive
Decatur, Georgia
404-377-0108

Morning Call Coffee Stand
4436 Veterans Boulevard
Metairie, Louisiana
    (suburban New Orleans)
504-779-5348

Shipley Do-Nuts
2151 South Lamar Avenue
Oxford, Mississippi
662-281-8414

Spudnut Shoppe
810 W. Faulkner Street
El Dorado, Arkansas
870-863-9914

MIDWEST

Moto
945 W. Fulton Market
Chicago, Illinois
312-491-0058

New Martha Washington
  Bakery
10335 Joseph Campau Street
Hamtramck, Michigan
313-872-1988

Oaza Bakery
11829 Joseph Campau Street
Hamtramck, Michigan
313-365-7010

Zingerman's Roadhouse
2501 Jackson Avenue
Ann Arbor, Michigan
734-663-3663

WEST

Agnes Bake Shop
46 Hoolai Street
Kailaua, Hawaii
808-262-5367

Bob's Coffee and Donuts
3 W. Fairfax Avenue
Los Angeles, California
323-933-8929

Champion Malassadas
1926 S. Beretania Street
Honolulu, Hawaii
808-947-8778

Chef Mavro
1969 S. King Street
Honolulu, Hawaii
808-944-4714

Donut Man
915 E. Route 66
Glendora, California
626-335-9111

Leonard's Bakery
933 Kapahulu Avenue
Honolulu, Hawaii
808-737-5591

Randy's Donuts
805 W. Manchester
   Boulevard
Inglewood, California
310-645-4707

Spudnut Shop
228 Williams Boulevard
Richland, Washington
509-943-3000

Stan's Donuts
10948 Weyburn Avenue
Los Angeles, California
310-208-8660

Tex Drive-In
45-690 Pakalana Street
Honokaa, Hawaii
808-775-0598

Top Pot
2124 Fifth Avenue
Seattle, Washington
206-728-1966

Voodoo Doughnuts and
   Wedding Chapel
22 S.W. Third Avenue
Portland, Oregon
503-241-4704

Thanks, Y'all

The good folks at Leroy Percy State Park, down in the Mississippi Delta, provided a hideout. Mary Beth Lasseter, my colleague at the Southern Foodways Alliance, made me look good. David Highfill, Sarah Landis, and Katie McKee at Putnam put my name in lights. Amy Evans danced around a vat of hot oil and shot beautiful photographs. Angie Mosier interpreted my scribblings and turned them into recipes. Lance Elko of *Attaché* gave me ink. So did Marika McEvoy of *Travel + Life*. David Black, my agent, was always by my side—even when he was half a world away hacking out messages on his Blackberry.

Dore Minatodani of the Hawaiian Collection at the University of Hawaii at Manoa shared donut trivia. Joan Namkoong of Honolulu talked *malassadas*. Rod Davis and Pete Wells taught me how to do the hula. William Woys Weaver of Philadelphia showed me the way to Little Pittsburgh. Jon Lyon clued me to

NyQuil donuts. Jan Longone and Ann Fowler at the University of Michigan dug deep for sources. Corby Kummer plotted Boston. Robb Walsh drove to the end of the earth (better known as the far reaches of the Houston exurbs) in search of churros. Robin Mower shared exacting research. Sandy Oliver published an issue of *Food History News* right when I needed it. Barbara Kuck fed me *zeppole*.

My time in the stacks revealed a number of gems, including "*Ich Bin ein Berliner*': Dunkers and Donuts in American Popular Culture" by James Deutsch, from the May 1994 edition of *Revue Française d'Études Américaines*. In making sense of New England foodways, I relied upon a number of books, including *America's Founding Food: The Story of New England Cooking* by Keith Stavely and Kathleen Fitzgerald. Sandy Oliver's book *Saltwater Foodways: New Englanders and Their Food, at Sea and at Ashore, in the Nineteenth Century*, also proved a boon.

A number of books on the Salvation Army proved helpful, especially *Red-Hot and Righteous: The Urban Religion of the Salvation Army* by Diane Winston and *Marching to Glory: The History of the Salvation Army in the United States of America, 1880–1980* by Edward McKinley. In writing on Cambodian-run donut shops, the reporting of the *Los Angeles Times* proved invaluable as did the documentary film *Cambodian Donut Dreams,* directed by Charles Davis.

As ever, my wife, Blair, read my words and called my bluffs. And my son, Jess, forgave my absences and was always game for a dozen. Thanks, y'all.

About the Author

John T. Edge is a contributing editor for *Gourmet* magazine and a longtime contributing writer for the *Oxford American*. He was the food columnist for *Attaché*, the US Airways in-flight magazine, and now serves as culinary curator for NPR's *Weekend Edition*. Edge's work for *Saveur* and other magazines has been featured in the last five editions of the *Best Food Writing* compilation. He was a 2004 finalist for the M. F. K. Fisher Distinguished Writing Award from the James Beard Foundation.

Edge has a number of books to his credit, including the James Beard Award–nominated *A Gracious Plenty: Recipes and Recollections from the American South* and *Southern Belly*, a mosaic-like portrait of Southern food told through profiles of people and places. He is general editor of the book series Cornbread Nation: The Best of Southern Food Writing, and foodways section editor for the forthcoming edition of the *Encyclopedia of Southern Culture.*

In addition, he is director of the Southern Foodways Alliance, an institute of the Center for the Study of Southern Culture at the University of Mississippi, where he dedicates his time to documenting and celebrating the diverse food cultures of the United States. In 2003, the *Financial Times* of London named Edge "One of Twenty Southerners to Watch," a distinction recognizing "Southerners whose achievements will have a greater impact in the future . . . on the national and international stage."

Edge lives in Oxford, Mississippi, with his son, Jess, and his wife, Blair Hobbs, a teacher and painter. His website is at www.johntedge.com.